UNSHACKLING THE TRUTH

Triumphant Over Injustice

by
Keith Tyrone Bush

Gotham Books

30 N Gould St.
Ste. 20820, Sheridan, WY 82801
https://gothambooksinc.com/

Phone: 1 (307) 464-7800

© 2024 *Keith Tyrone Bush*. All rights reserved.

No part of this book may be reproduced, stored in a retrieval system, or transmitted by any means without the written permission of the author.

Published by Gotham Books (August 1, 2024)

ISBN: 979-8-88775-836-7 (H)
ISBN: 979-8-88775-834-3 (P)
ISBN: 979-8-88775-835-0 (E)

Because of the dynamic nature of the Internet, any web addresses or links contained in this book may have changed since publication and may no longer be valid.

The views expressed in this work are solely those of the author and do not necessarily reflect the views of the publisher, and the publisher hereby disclaims any responsibility for them.

DEDICATION

To Sherese Watson and the truth.

To all those incarcerated for a crime they did not commit.

To those who achieved the goal of exoneration after a relentless pursuit. To all innocence project attorneys, staff, students, conviction integrity units and other concerned persons who work to exonerate the innocent, with specific reference to my attorney Adele Bernhard and her students.

To my family and friends who believed and supported me. To all defense witnesses for telling the truth and those who have come forward with the truth.

To my late Queen Mother of North Bellport, Mrs. Rae Maynes, for her love and support.

A special dedication to my wife, Dora Moore Bush, for believing in me and teaching me how to love again.

CONTENTS

DEDICATION III
PREFACE VI
WHEN THE RAIN FALLS 1
THE SENSELESS MURDER 6
FALSE ACCUSATIONS 12
SUFFOLK COUNTY JAIL 21
THE TRIAL 44
THE VERDICT 60
LIFE IMPRISONMENT 65
THE YEAR 1976 70
PREPARING FOR THE UNKNOWN 79
GHOSTS OF ATTICA 87
PSEUDO-GODS IN BLACK ROLES 92
DEVELOPMENTS AFTER TRIAL 99
SPECIAL HOUSING UNIT 102
THE ALLURE OF CRIMINAL BEHAVIOR 114
THE GREEN HAVEN EXPERIENCE 119
THE DNA DILEMMA 134
THE WORST CRIME OF ALL 143
GOD, THE HOLY BIBLE, AND THE TRIAL OATH 152
WHO KILLED SHERESE WATSON: THE SEARCH FOR CLOSURE 165
THE CONFESSION TAKERS 197
PRIVILEGED STATUS OVER ACCOUNTABILITY 212

EXONERATION	224
THE BIRTH OF A MOVEMENT	235
RESURRECTION: THE EMPOWERMENT MODEL	247
THE EMPOWERMENT JOURNEY	257
CREATING MY OWN REALITY	266
MAPPING OUT THE PROCESS	269
THE PURGING PROCESS	275
SPIRITUAL ENHANCEMENT	278
PERSONAL DEVELOPMENT	279
SENSE OF COMMUNITY	280
CONSTRUCTING A NEW LIFE	282
A SELF-EMPOWERMENT TRANSFORMATION SAMPLE	289
WHAT FREEDOM REALLY FEELS LIKE	293
PHOTO GALLERY	297

PREFACE

Imagine having lived the first seventeen years of your life as a content, carefree young teenager, then suddenly being kidnapped and held captive inside one prison cage after another for over three decades. Imagine enduring this for something you had absolutely nothing to do with.

Imagine being trapped in that hell until you are forty-nine, never having had the opportunity to experience life as a free adult, free of incarceration. Imagine the eternity of each month slowly stretching before you. Each day. Each hour. Each minute.

Imagine being mentally trained by confinement to perceive society as a world "out there." If not for prison transfers or media outlets, you would have no idea that the world outside of prison really exists. Try to imagine living with your sole desire being the prospect of someday returning to that outside world, with your ultimate fear being dying in prison.

If you can imagine some of these things, it may give you an inkling about who I am and why I had to tell my story.

My story is intimately connected to a tragedy. It involved the death of another human being. Although I was convicted of this crime, this version of the story is also about my own victimization—how I was abused by the criminal justice system and was robbed of over four decades of my life.

Over forty-four years ago, the community of North Bellport, New York was shocked by a senseless murder that has lingered in memory for decades. When the media reported details of the incident, I too was stunned and saddened. However, two days later, I was tricked into police custody, not allowed to speak with anyone, forced to sign a statement, arrested, and charged for this same murder.

Fifteen months after my arrest, in what was the longest deliberation trial in Suffolk County history at that time, I was found guilty. I was given a sentence of twenty years to life in prison with four years to run concurrently. It was the first time I was ever involved with the judicial system, and as you will learn, I am the devastating proof that the young, innocent, and vulnerable can be condemned while the guilty go free.

To write my story, I had to revisit some painful experiences from the past. My deepest fears, sorrows, hurt, anger, and resentments were challenged by my determination to survive. For the first time in my life, I would come face to face with many conflicting forces battling to control my mind. There are no joyful emotions to embrace in a journey filled with so much pain.

But my journey also provided some valuable lessons.

As I attempted to extract the most significant elements of this encounter, I became more and more aware of the impact this whole experience had upon me. I was surprised to discover that what I thought would be a simple expedition into the past was a pathway connecting my past behaviors with unresolved conflicts. I discovered how these behavior patterns affected the way I interacted with the world.

Over time, my internal conflicts became fused with anguish. At some point, these raging hostilities revealed a need to address deeper levels of my psyche. The process I chose was difficult, but it had a healing effect. In this book, I also reveal that process. My efforts to explore and cleanse the inner core of my being would become my most significant pilgrimage.

Waking up in a jail cell was a disorienting and demanding experience for an unsophisticated teenager. At the age of seventeen, I had virtually no exposure to, and very little knowledge of, the world outside the microcosm that defined my existence. Despite grief, fear, confusion, death threats, and the loss of the best years of my life, prison would become the place where I would transition from a boy into a man.

I felt suppressed. I became introverted. However, I also learned to be highly aware of my surroundings. It was from this inward-focused perspective that I learned a lot about myself, including better ways to improve myself and to operate more effectively—both subjectively and in my relationships with the things around me. I was determined to rise above the many negative activities associated with prison life. I vowed to fight for my freedom, to empower myself, and to survive.

You will read in this book how I endured in an abnormal environment. I will take you through this world. I will tell you how I had to carve out my own space after learning the first rule of prison: Only the strong survive. My personal identity and worldview were shattered. I will reveal the process I undertook to transform it.

My life in prison involved a multitude of experiences. I will attempt to highlight those that concern the purpose of my conviction and transformation.

If I could have foreseen my life as it has unfolded, I would not have chosen to live it. If I had the power to foresee this tragedy and my suffering, and if giving my life could have saved the victim and prevented it, I would gladly have done so. The victim did not deserve it, and I did not deserve to live in this world in so much pain.

My relationship with the criminal justice system has left me with absolutely no confidence in it. You may wonder why then would I appeal to the same system in which I had no faith? The truth is that I had no other alternatives. If I had not exonerated myself through the courts, I would never have experienced a life of true freedom.

The criminal justice system has been prejudiced against me in every way conceivable. Even the New York State Division of Parole frowned upon my innocence, acting as if their system was infallible. After rendering all my efforts irrelevant, they denied me parole on six separate occasions (twenty-four months each time, the maximum allowed, amounting to twelve additional years past the court-imposed sentence of twenty years to life).

Then, unexpectedly, I was quietly pushed out of the prison system without ever meeting the two major requirements for my release. In this book, I will tell you the reason why.

During the twelve years I spent on parole, the possibility remained that I could have ended up dying in prison. The harsh lifetime parole restrictive conditions imposed upon me made it more difficult to transition from prison and continue to fight for exoneration. My life had been locked into the sentencing remarks of New York state Suffolk County's trial judge, Melvin Tanenbaum, who said, "The real tragedy in this case is that two young lives have been abbreviated."

Those words would hold true for over forty-four-plus years of suffering until finally I was given my life back. No longer is my life an abbreviation but a new beginning that stands upon the foundation of exoneration.

When The Rain Falls

Water is the Earth's bloodstream. Oceans, rivers, lakes, streams and deep reservoirs function like the heart, veins, and tiny arterial vessels that transport our human blood, cleansing and nurturing life.

The human body and the Earth are composed similarly of around two-thirds water. The view from space of Earth's massive, blue, watery, and white-clouded sphere is one of the most glorious scenes to be viewed by any observer with the ability to peek into this corner of the universe.

The great oceans, waterfalls, and rivers are never still but fixed in a continuum.

When waterfalls, as on a warm summer day, there is nothing like holding hands, kissing, and walking in the rain with the one you love. Moving water always puts on an intriguing performance as it dances.

But water can be a swinging pendulum, too. When unleashed, it can cause as much destruction as any other force on the planet. It will not discriminate. Water bows only to Mother Nature. It will drown or destroy anything that attempts to upset nature's need for balance and cleansing.

In time, water's persistent power can turn mountains into mud slides; cause colossal land masses to sink or rise; can split apart or break into pieces any of the Earth's continents. Time is always on its side.

How is it that all the events that define my life and all my near-death encounters are associated with water? Water has drowned me in some of my most vivid nightmares. In many ways, water has and will always remain my deepest fear.

I attribute these fears to several nightmares I had at different times in my life. In each of those nightmares, I found myself struggling between waking up and drowning.

My relationship with water began with my earliest recollection when I was three years old. My mother was bathing me in the sink. I remember the strong sense of fear caused by this strange substance that cleansed my tiny body. While my mother held my body firmly upright, I was trying to get out of the way of the water. Could it have been my fear of water that preserved my recollection of that event?

Another incident occurred when I burned my left arm with hot water. After my cousin boiled hot dogs for us, I volunteered to pour the hot water in the sink. I wasn't tall enough to reach and had to use a chair. I lost my footing and almost fell off the chair while trying to transfer the hot water from the stove to the sink. My left arm was burned. I was fortunate—if I had fallen completely off the chair, the outcome could have been disastrous.

Once, while roaming the community with friends on our way to Pleasure Beach, an island near the coast of Bridgeport, Connecticut, we stopped on the bridge where men fished. We approached an older man who was putting away his belongings. We asked him to twirl his fishing string around in the air. We bugged him until he agreed to do it just one time. He warned us to back up.

Everyone backed up to create the space he demanded, but I didn't move as fast as the others. When the man turned around to twirl the fishing string in the air, the string's hook ripped through my flesh, from the bottom of my chin to the left side of my lip. It was a deep cut that healed into a nasty scar.

When I was fourteen, two older White guys encouraged two of my younger cousins and me to take a boat ride with them down a narrow brook. At one point, they started rocking the boat in a way that scared us. One of the older guys tried to grab one of my cousins and throw him in the water.

I managed to push the older guy out of the canoe while the boat was rocking back and forth. At the same time, my cousins and I jumped out of the canoe, making our way to land. The guy who fell in the water screamed to his friend to "get that nigger over there, drown his ass!"

He was referring to me.

My cousins were far better swimmers than me and made it to land first. As soon as I reached the shore, the three of us took off running toward home. The two guys chose not to pursue us. We could hear them laughing at us as we fled in fear for our lives. They may not have been serious about drowning any of us, but we had no way of knowing.

We often played baseball near the same brook, located in the back of a school. One day while playing, we smelled a foul odor but paid no attention until the ball was hit over the fence and rolled down to the bank of the brook. When one of my cousins went to get the ball, he discovered a dead body lying in the lake.

That was the first time I had ever seen a dead body. It terrified us. I later discovered the dead person was the brother of the man who had accidentally cut me in the face with a fishing hook.

One night in Bridgeport, when I was fifteen, I was walking to the other side of town to visit family members and a girlfriend. As I was walking across one of the bridges that served as an entrance to downtown, two Latino men, apparently high on drugs or alcohol, tried to grab me, pick me up, and throw me over the bridge into the water. I surely would have drowned.

I fought with them and managed to break free and run to the other side of the bridge.

When I was sixteen, my father, a truck driver, saved my life in a tractor-trailer accident. I was traveling with him down I-95 on the way home from work. It started raining extremely hard. While I slept on the passenger's side, another tractor-trailer hit us from behind, causing both trucks to lose control.

A gas station and roadway were directly below and slightly ahead of us. Both trucks began jack-knifing as the drivers tried to regain control. All I remembered was my father screaming out my name as he worked the wheel of his truck.

I woke up from a daze to my father yelling at me to "Watch out!"

Instinctively, I turned to look out the window. At the same time, I felt my father reach out, grabbing and pulling me on top of him while trying to control the truck with his other hand. In that moment, the other truck smashed into the passenger side where I had been seated. The impact drove our truck down a bank just beyond the gas station and roadway. Miraculously, no one was hurt. The next day, we drove by the company to view the damage.

It was obvious that if my father had not grabbed me when he did, I would have instantly died.

Why has water always been present at or connected to my most frightening experiences? Even today, when I'm around water, I sometimes wonder if this substance will ultimately cause my demise. Or will it swing like a pendulum and begin in these latter years of my existence to define the victorious unraveling of my fate?

The Senseless Murder

In the early morning hours of Saturday, January 11, 1975, a young teenage girl was murdered while raindrops sprinkled over North Bellport, a hamlet in the town of Brookhaven on Long Island. As the darkness approached daylight, rain began to pour more heavily. It would continue off and on throughout the day and into the evening.

The girl's name was Sherese Watson.

Bellport is located on the shore of Bellport Bay, an arm of the Great South Bay. It consists of two sections. Its southern side is "The Village" and the northern side "North Bellport." Train tracks run parallel with the Montauk Highway, an east-west road that extends over thirty miles across the southern shore of Long Island. This road along the train tracks divides the two halves.

In the 1970s, the main road in the village section consisted of shops, a deli, and restaurants. The village, referred to by some as "a hidden gem of Long Island," also took pride in its community. At that time, the village's populace was predominately White. Like all parts of the United States, White people in the village enjoyed a privileged status over their Black northern counterparts. This was particularly true in how the neighborhoods were policed.

I lived in the predominantly Black section on the northern side of Bellport in 1975. In those days, North Bellport was a small, close-knit community. Although the disparities between the Black and White populace in Bellport were apparent, most people in

North Bellport were also hard-working citizens. They took pride in taking care of their personal property and environment.

North Bellport in those days was experiencing an influx of population, largely from the South, with a sprinkling of newcomers from nearby towns and New York City.

In the early 1970s, Bellport was known for its house parties and social events. Bellport teenagers were introduced to a party lifestyle early on.

I met Sherese in the fall of 1974 around the start of the school year. I usually started school in Bellport and spent my summer months in Bridgeport with my father. In 1973, I reversed the pattern and went to high school in Bridgeport. A year later, I returned to Bellport to start the eleventh grade.

Sherese was introduced to me by a friend named Stephinie Sheffey. Stephinie and I had a close friendship. We were born one week apart, had been in some of the same classes at school, associated with most of the same people and even hung out together on occasions.

I did not know Sherese very well because she was not in my immediate circle. But when our paths did cross Sherese was always down to earth, open-minded, and friendly toward me. Sherese was spontaneous and full of laughter. She got a kick out of talking, partying, having fun, and teasing people.

Sherese once told me she had moved to Bellport from New York City. She talked proudly about New York City life.

On one occasion. I stopped by Stephinie to get my hair braided and Sherese was there and braided it instead. Sherese seen me at another Bellport party, prior to this incident, and asked me to enter a dance contest with her. Sherese was a good person.

At around nine a.m. on that tragic Saturday, Sherese's mother, a girl I had recently met named Brenda Carlos, and Sissy Williams came by my house looking for Sherese. I had no idea of her whereabouts. I had last talked with her at a party the night before. Since I didn't know where she was, they left.

At four p.m. that same day, Sherese's parents, Brenda, and two police came to my house, again looking for her. The situation seemed more serious. After they questioned me again and left, I called one of Sherese's best friends, but she wasn't home.

That evening, I met up with three of my friends. I told them Sherese didn't go home the night before and that her mother and the police had come to my house inquiring about her. We only discussed it briefly; at that point none of us in our wildest dreams would guess Sherese had been murdered.

The four of us stopped by a store, then went to a party at 735 Bourdois Avenue. This was the same house where I'd attended a party the night before—the last time I had seen Sherese.

I stayed there the second night with my friends until almost one a.m. before one of my friends and I headed home.

The rain had begun to sprinkle lightly again in the evening. It would continue until morning of the next day, Sunday. It wasn't until that afternoon, after the rain had dissipated, that Sherese Watson's body was discovered.

The weather was warmer than normal for this time of year. Like many other people, I went out to enjoy some of the sun's warmth. Monday would be a school day, so I wanted to take advantage of the nice weather.

I was in Bellport's Park playing basketball with friends when we heard a siren. We didn't take the sound seriously until someone else drove past the park on their way to a crime scene, yelling at us about the shocking news that a dead body had been discovered in a vacant lot.

The body was in a lot with houses on both sides, behind the foundation of a church under construction. It was a short distance from the intersection of Meade and Brookhaven avenues.

The four of us stopped playing basketball, gathered our things, and ran to the scene along with three other passersby. Little did we know we would soon be overwhelmed by the horror of the single most shocking tragedy to hit the Bellport community up to that point.

Crowds of people gathered. Detectives and news reporters conducted interviews as people roamed the outskirts of the roped-off section where the body of a young Bellport High School student lay under a white cloth.

The first report I heard when I arrived was that the deceased had holes in her back and had been killed with a shotgun. There were also rumors she had last been seen leaving Friday night's house party in a red car with some boys from the nearby town of Riverhead.

Seeing Sherese's body lying on the ground, covered, and cordoned off by rope, was one of the most frightening and saddest things I had ever witnessed.

My sadness became one with the sadness of the growing crowd as a horrible reality continued to sink in. Fear of the unknown quickly turned this quiet village of North Bellport into a nightmare.

I knew the deceased and had interacted with her shortly before her murder, so I left the scene feeling empty and confused, wondering, *how could anyone do something like this, and who did it?* Like some people in the community, I felt the need to help in any way I could. I felt hurt for Sherese. I think all of us who knew her did.

Unbeknownst to me, I became a "person of interest" based on reports of my interaction with the victim on her last night alive. I don't believe police or news reporters initially knew who I was, because no one approached me for an interview at the scene about my activities, recollection of events, or any other assistance I could offer.

The same night, my cousin, George Gholson, came to my house with a few friends and a man named Robert Stewart. I had never met Stewart and knew nothing about him. He introduced himself as a concerned community citizen with a genuine interest in young people.

I went with the group to Stewart's house. There, he discussed the incident. Stewart told us he was trying to get some boys together to help find out who'd committed this terrible crime. He asked us if we would help. We agreed.

I felt emotionally bound to help. I had been brought up to believe helping was what I was supposed to do.

When I returned home that Sunday night, my mother told me detectives had come by and called several times to interview me. They asked if she would keep me home from school to be interviewed at nine a.m. the next day.

My mother questioned me about what I knew. When I went to bed, I got very little sleep. As things continued to sink in, I kept waking up, lying in bed thinking about what had happened, periodically wiping tears away from my eyes.

False Accusations

My mother kept me home from school on January 13th so I could be interviewed by detectives. Two detectives came to my house and asked to speak to me alone. Initially, my mother didn't agree with that plan, but I assured her it was all right. I didn't have anything to hide. She told me she wanted to see any statement before I signed it.

I sat in the detectives' car in the driveway and told them all I could remember about my activities on the night of the murder. They wrote it down. I signed the statement without reading it. They thanked me, I got out of the car, and went back inside my house.

My mother asked me what happened. I told her, and she had a fit because I hadn't let her read the statement before I signed it. I remember her telling me I better not ever do anything like that again without her knowing.

Later that evening, I went with some friends back to Robert Stewart's house. We discussed the situation further. I still didn't detect Stewart's ulterior intentions at that point. Like a fool, I continued to place my trust in his hands.

News of the crime started to gain local and national attention. The county newspaper, *Newsday*, ran a front-page cover story. In that story I was mentioned as one of the last people with Sherese. The reporter wrote I couldn't be found for comment. The article implied that I was a person of interest in the murder. The story also mentioned Sherese's interaction with some boys from Riverhead in a stolen red car.

Homicide detectives, meanwhile, were feeling the pressure of taking on a task that involved over a hundred people, with a plethora of suspects and little cooperation from anyone.

Many parents—mostly single mothers—kept their children from talking for fear of retribution. This slowed the investigation even as the media mounted their pressures.

The house party became the focal point of the investigation.

I had told detectives at my home the same story I would later tell under oath. I had attended that party, where I met up with a friend named Chuckie Corbin. We stayed at the party for close to an hour and then left for my house a few blocks away to get some food.

On our way, Tom Davis, Junie Scruggs, and a third person I didn't know were walking just ahead of us. The three of them were going to Tom's house, around the corner from where I lived. We caught up with them, traveled in the same direction, and agreed to meet up to return to the party.

Chuckie and I ate, then picked up Tom and Junie (the third person did not return). The four of us walked back to the party, arriving a little after eleven p.m. Chuckie decided to leave early—about fifteen minutes after our arrival.

Lenora Hart was at the party, but she had a curfew. Sometime after eleven p.m., her mother came to pick her up. Moments later, Lenora came back inside the house to ask me if I would talk to her mother so that she could stay at the party past her curfew.

Lenora wanted to stay because her boyfriend was there and knew I was the only person at the party with whom her mother would allow her to remain. Lenora and I walked outside to speak with her mother. I agreed to keep an eye on her and promised to see to it that she got home safely.

That was when I first saw Sherese. We spoke briefly outside. She asked questions, like who was inside and if the party was crowded. Sherese also introduced me to Brenda Carlos.

After our conversation, Sherese and Brenda went inside. Before I reentered, I spoke with Tom, who was outside smoking. I told him to let me know when they were ready to leave. I reentered the party sometime around midnight.

I stayed inside, engaging in small talk with Lenora, her boyfriend Gary Watkins, his brother Chris, and Junie. I listened to the live three-piece band. Brenda had taken a seat, while Sherese danced on a few occasions and conversed with friends. I periodically scanned my surroundings, secretly hoping a girl named Barbara Girtman would show up.

At one point, Sherese walked over to me and asked, "Why are you so quiet? You're usually dancing."

I told her I was just checking out the band and watching everyone else dance. I said that the band played well.

"Yeah, they play all right," she replied.

I asked Sherese who one of the teens she was dancing with was, but she didn't know his name.

Sherese talked with Lenora and danced again before talking with me a second time. We were engaged in conversation when Brenda walked up to her, said something, and left. I asked Sherese what Brenda had said, and she told me Brenda was going home. I assumed Brenda and Sherese were cousins until she told me that

Brenda lived in Bellport with her aunt. Sherese explained that her relationship with Brenda went back to New York City.

Sherese danced one last time and continued to talk with friends. Five or ten minutes later, she said, "I'll see you later, Keefie."

And she walked out the front door.

It would be the last time I would see her alive.

When Sherese left, I didn't get the impression she was going home. Just about everyone was coming and going freely in and out of the party throughout the night for fresh air and other purposes. I didn't see her leave with anyone.

I stayed at the party listening to the band and talking for about two more hours. I remained in the company of six people, with approximately thirty other people coming and going, until about three a.m. I never left the party during that time. Finally, Sissy told me her boyfriend was leaving and was ready to take her home. Right after they left, I left with Tom and Junie.

When we stepped outside the party, we saw Kevin Brame. He was trying to start his car and asked for our help. The four of us tried to push the car but it wouldn't start. Calvin Lynch happened to be driving by. He asked Kevin what was wrong. He told us to get in and gave us a push. The car started. Kevin took me home first. I arrived after three a.m.

I attended school on January 14th, the day after the detectives had come by.

This would be the day my life would change forever.

I will never forget the feeling of being an outcast, particularly in the presence of some of my closest friends and those who knew me. The *Newsday* article gave students the right to view me with suspicion.

Everywhere I walked, the air was stifling, laden with a lonely and quiet emptiness. I caught a few eyes peeking at me and quickly looking away. For the first time, I began to think, *maybe some of these people think I did this.*

Although my name was mentioned in the papers, I didn't know detectives had received a statement the previous day from a girl named Maxine Bell. The detectives hadn't released that information to the media or anyone else. Because of her statement, they were already aggressively pursuing me, already in the process of luring me into custody.

At around noon that day, my cousin, and a friend came to Bellport Senior High School to tell me Stewart wanted to see me at his house at one p.m. and that a couple of his friends would be there.

The assistant principal, Leslie Manigault, approached us as we were conversing in the hall. He told us I would not be allowed to leave school early unless I was released by an adult. Stewart returned with my cousin and friend and had me released from school.

Upon our arrival at Stewart's house, two policemen came downstairs. The police started asking a lot of questions about the boys in the red car, saying they had their names on a list along with other names—none of which they could identify. However, they said this information was at the police station. They asked me if I would show them where a student lived who we all agreed might have pertinent information about the boys from the red car.

I thought I was doing the right thing. I had no idea the investigation had zeroed in on me. I didn't even know police were involved in a larger scheme to lure me into their possession and hand me over to vicious homicide detectives.

Looking back at the seventeen-year-old me, as shameful as it is to admit, I had to have been the most ignorant person in the world for placing my trust in law enforcement. This would become the second biggest mistake I ever made in my life.

Instead of taking me back to Stewart's home, I was taken to a basement in a local precinct, where I was placed incommunicado. I was handed over to detectives Dennis Rafferty and August Stahl for intense interrogation.

At the precinct, the detectives immediately tried to get me to sign a statement admitting to Sherese's murder. I repeatedly insisted I didn't commit the crime.

Now I was feeling a different kind of pressure. I didn't want to help or talk anymore. I just wanted to go home. I had been tricked. I felt betrayed and trapped. I was under police control.

I kept telling the detectives the same thing: I did not kill Sherese. After it became clear they didn't want to hear that, I then started telling them I wanted to call my mother. Each time I asked, they refused. Instead, they kept trying to pressure me into admitting guilt.

After an hour of these unsuccessful tactics, the two detectives took me to Long Island's main homicide squad in Hauppauge.

At the homicide squad, detectives took me to a small room and sat me in a chair, where I remained from three p.m. until sometime after eleven p.m. One, two, or three detectives questioned me at a time. Their questioning involved deception, persuasion, pressure, good-cop-bad-cop tactics, intimidation, and other methods of manipulation.

At around ten-thirty, five or six detectives rushed into the room and grabbed me from all sides, pinning me in the chair. They started hitting me on the top of the head with a large phone book.

Every time I struggled to get loose, detective Rafferty kicked me in the groin. He stopped only to warn me to sign the statement and threatened to continue torturing me if I didn't. Each time I refused; they repeated the process.

After about five rounds of abuse, I was helpless. I felt powerless, unable to free or defend myself. I was frustrated and confused. I started to cry, but it was to no avail. They showed no mercy.

Detective Rafferty led the way. He kicked me harder in the groin. The other detectives savored their actions, as if it was business as usual.

It must have been, because on the outside of that room, everyone present knew what was happening to me but didn't care or intervene.

Rafferty said things like, "I'll make sure you never have any kids if you don't sign this statement, you hear me!"

His words were always backed up by one or two powerful kicks directly to my genitals.

Once they convinced me that they were going to make me sterile, I became exacerbated by terror and fear. I was consumed with the idea that if I didn't stop them, I would never be able to have kids.

It was at that point that I broke down. I was unprepared for this type of torture. I had never been so defenseless and confused in all my life.

I signed and initialed the papers, which I didn't read and were never read to me.

But the detectives denied me the right to call my mother. I was placed under arrest and charged with murder.

I still had no idea of the magnitude of what I had just done. I was totally ignorant of the criminal justice system.

I didn't believe they could keep me in jail. All I had to do was tell them what the detectives did to me, and I would get out the next day. They couldn't put me in jail for signing a piece of paper, right? I didn't even know what the paper said.

I would, of course, not get out the next day. I would spend over three decades of my life in a cage. By signing that statement, I surrendered to fear, and fear sent me straight to hell.

It would become the worst decision in my entire life. A decision that would become more painful because it was a decision I could never take back. One I would have made differently even if it meant dying for it.

Signing that statement was by far my greatest shame!

My encounter with the homicide squad changed my life forever. For many years, I found it difficult to articulate. Pain, grief, and rage would sometimes consume me. For a long time, it seemed more expedient to hide the experience in my subconscious.

Each time I look back at that encounter, I feel like a fool. How could I be so weak and naive? Why was I so confused? It seems obvious now that when I signed that statement, I was telling the world I accepted the blame for the death of this young girl.

I feel now as if I should have suffered whatever consequences would have come from maintaining a strong moral stance. I knew I could have withstood far more pain. Instead, I gave in to my fear.

Suffolk County Jail

The next day, I stood with a lawyer before the district court to be arraigned for intentional murder. The judge asked my lawyer if my parents were present. He allowed my mother to stand with me before the court, probably because of my age, even though there were no laws that mandated it during police interrogations.

As my mother approached me, she saw me and asked, "What did they do to you?"

It was too late. I was disappointed when I found out I wasn't going home. My lawyer emphasized to us not to talk about the case with anyone as we departed for what would become the worst experience in my life.

That first day is seared into my memory. I was escorted past one tier of Suffolk County jail to the opposite side, where I was directed to enter a cage. The authoritative sound of bars opening and closing went hand in hand with the corresponding sounds of a few shouted threats against my life and the tough guy faces on some defendants.

As I approached the inside of the tier, my mind shifted to the lineal arrangement of what looked like a succession of animal cages. I had never been inside a jail or prison (aside from the small holding pen the night before), so I found the initial exposure of this structure intimidating.

In less than twenty-four hours, I was moved to an isolated location called sick bay. It was a small area consisting of about four cells. Outside of the cells was a television and a guard station with round-the-clock observation and security. Except for showers, visits, medical and court appointments, those of us in sick bay were locked in with no recreation or privacy.

Locked next to me was a man on high doses of medication. He slept most of the time. Locked two cells down was Ronald Defeo, Jr., who was accused of killing his entire family, including his young siblings, in what became known as the Amityville Horror case. He often talked to the guards about the particularities of his case. I couldn't help but listen in on their conversations. I remember trying to digest the seriousness of his predicament.

I followed the advice of my lawyer and never spoke to him or the guards about my case during my stay at sick bay. Defeo's lawyer should have given him the same advice. During his trial, these same guards came forward and falsified testimony against him.

I started having periodic pulsating headaches. I brought it to the attention of the nurses and doctor at my first examination. I was always given aspirin and told the headaches were stress related. I went along with what I was told and took the aspirin.

I was worried about the headaches for a few months, until eventually they went away.

For years, I would think about that night at the precinct. *Damn, I use to think to myself, I hope they didn't fuck me up*! Detective Rafferty would appear in my mind with the threat of sterilization.

Initially, I couldn't understand why I was being viewed by others as if I was some freak in a sideshow each time I was escorted from my cell. I didn't realize I'd been separated from the general population. There were other detainees accused of murder and treated no differently than the rest, so I assumed it was based on the threats I had heard earlier. It wasn't until a few days into my incarceration that I would find out the truth.

In sick bay, I was becoming bored watching television all day. I decided to read some of the old newspapers stacked up on the table. It gave me a way to pass the time.

Being sports oriented, I turned to the back page and worked my way to the front, looking at the pictures and half read articles I found most interesting. As I backwardly reached the front section of one of the pages, I was caught by total surprise!

I just could not believe what I had done to myself. I read and re-read what one of the papers said: "...a signed confession from Keith Bush in which he admits stabbing and strangling the deceased when she fought off his sexual advances..."

The paper also mentioned tiny puncture wounds on Sherese's lower back and bruises on her face. My heart started beating like crazy. I sat on my bed in a state of disbelief and shock. I felt like I was dying on the inside. It was the worst feeling I'd felt in my entire life.

There was something about the way in which Sherese had been murdered that deeply affected me. Reading my name attached to this crime opened my eyes for the first time. I could not believe the way detectives had diabolically implicated me in the crime.

Based on rumors I'd heard at the crime scene; I was under the impression Sherese had been shot in the back. She had been stabbed some thirty-something times by what was alleged to be a metal afro-pick, which left almost a hundred tiny puncture wounds in her lower back.

Now I knew why I was trapped in hell and viewed by others the way I was. From that moment, I had to come to terms with the seriousness of my predicament, as well as what had really happened to Sherese.

As I thought about how she was killed and the way police connected me to the crime, I got a strange feeling, as if the whole world were looking down on me. So, *this* was what everyone was thinking I did? Shame invaded my entire being like a spreading cancer.

I tried but could not stop the tears from welling up. I thought about my family and friends, to no avail. For the first time in my life, I felt alone. There I was, locked in a cage. I retreated into a psychological shell. I would find comfort there for many years.

That night, I laid in bed, completely lost. My body felt numb from shame. I put the covers over my head and cried myself to sleep. The guard heard me and came to my cell to ask if I was all right. I ignored him.

I went to sleep feeling so out of control that I slept until almost four p.m. the next day. For three days, I hid in the dream state as I slept, and bowed to my fears, hurt, and shame. These were the first three emotions that rattled me at my core as they competed for control of my will.

The more I slept (hid), the more this deep state of depression engulfed me. On the third day, I opened my eyes, rose from my bed, and started doing push-ups. It was almost as if I needed to go there for cleansing and revitalization in preparation for a long and difficult journey.

I would remain in sick bay for about six weeks. I was then transferred to segregation.

Segregation was twenty-three-hour confinement with an hour-long recreation period on the gallery. Showers, shaves, or usage of the slop-sink were included within the recreation period.

It took a while for me to open. I did finally begin communicating with an older guy everyone called "Spade."

Spade was locked in the cell next to mine and did most of the talking. Our cells were directly in front of the television.

Spade was one of the guys placed in segregation for disciplinary reasons. He was a fighter and troublemaker against the administration.

I was unaware of terms like sick bay, the box, and segregation. I had no perception of jail other than the stories I was told and what I saw on television. Spade explained those things to me, as well as how the tier system operated.

We discussed the reasons I had been placed in segregation. He continually warned me about the seriousness of threats. I told him I understood why most people felt the way they did. It was because of what they read.

He would reply with things like, "That's bullshit! How can they accept stories from the media as true when those motherfuckers lie all the time? They all know how brutal police are in Suffolk County. They complain all day about what the police did to them, but when you make the same complaints, because of what you were arrested for, now they find it so hard to believe."

Spade was bold. He would tell me things like, "Besides, look at you—you ain't nothing but a fuckin' kid. You damn sure ain't no criminal. Do you know how many full-grown so-called hardcore criminals walking around here are fighting coerced confessions?"

He was the one who explained to me what a confession was and how bad I had fucked-up by signing one. He told me I wasn't going home anytime soon and warned me that, outside of a miracle, my fate had been sealed. He said my biggest mistake was trusting the police. He said under no circumstances were we to trust or help, as he put it, "those motherfuckin' devils."

This older man was surprised to learn how ignorant I was about what I had just gone through—and what I was about to go through. He felt kids like me were particularly vulnerable because nobody was teaching young people that police have always been enemies to black communities.

His messages were vivid. Listening to him made me feel even more like a fool for the decision I'd made. But it helped me to realize I had to come to terms with my new reality. He placed me face to face with the inadequacies I would have to overcome.

When I found out I could transfer out of segregation, I asked Spade to show me how. Initially, he tried to persuade me not to do it. But he eventually realized how persistent I was. Spade wrote a letter for me to submit to the administrators. Based on that letter and a personal interview, I won the right to be taken out of segregation and moved back into the general population.

The day I left; Spade told me not to talk with anyone about my case. "They'll end up testifying against you or gossip behind your back like little bitches." I could sense he was afraid for me when he told me not to hesitate to fight for respect.

I sometimes wonder why he took an interest in that lonely and confused boy. Why was he trying to rebuild my self-esteem and restore my confidence? Was it to prepare me for what the system had in store? He pulled no punches. I now realize he was preparing me for an even more oppressive storm.

I was lucky in many ways. The first card jail dealt to me was an ace of Spade. He opened my eyes to a lot of things about which I was entirely unaware. He viewed me as a young, vulnerable, and naive kid in water above his head. Spade was a straight shooter. And he never hesitated to pull the trigger.

This was my first introduction to hard-core wisdom. The best way to describe it is by what I overheard another prisoner say years later: "It's a dog-eat-dog world. It's not the dog with the fastest start; the dog with the loudest bark; or the dog that plays the best part. It's the dog with the coldest heart that gets the bone."

When I transferred to the general population, I knew no one in the gallery I was sent to. I moved freely about my business as if everything was normal.

Had Spade or any of the older guys sent word to leave me alone? Surely, if anyone wanted to jump me, there was little I could do. I was about five feet, four inches tall and a hundred and twenty pounds soaking wet. I had no allies and was outnumbered.

That didn't mean I was afraid to fight. I wasn't backing down to nobody. It was one of the things that bothered me so much. For decades, I was haunted by my own cowardliness for letting those detectives force me into submission. In time, that shame would become my rage.

It wasn't long before I had my first battle. I didn't initiate it, but it was an easy victory. The other guys seemed more impressed than me. During my stay at the county jail, I would have my fair share of fights.

Fighting always led to being forcibly escorted to the "Box," with physical abuse accompanying each trip. Three six-foot-plus, two hundred and fifty-pound-plus guards approached the cell door in riot gear. They were called the Doom Squad. The sergeant accompanying the Doom Squad carried a spray can of mace. Refusal to be handcuffed inside the cell would earn you a spraying.

One guard carried a mattress as a shield. The other guards would get behind him and the three would charge the cell, forcibly knocking you down, subduing and handcuffing you and then dragging you to the Box. Most beat-ups took place in the elevator or in the cell inside the Box. As a result of my trips there, I started developing the same kind of hatred for prison guards as I had for detectives.

The harsh treatment by guards triggered in me a feeling of déjà vu. I couldn't interpret that feeling until years later, when my mistreatment in prison by authorities became one and the same with the feelings I felt while studying the history of my ancestors concerning their mistreatment during slavery.

The Box had its own distinct qualities.

It had a formidable aura of despair, leaving the night hours thick with a hollow desolation. It had a way of dictating one's moods; it could not only drive a weak mind to depression but could force it into total submission. These conditions intensified as the number of those confined decreased or when all verbal communication in the late-night hours ceased.

During quiet times in the Box, the past had a way of transcending its own boundaries of space and time and reemerging through the legacy of writing that covered the cell walls. One could read the hubris and thirst for recognition.

"Big Mike was here and now he's gone. He left his name to carry on."

There were also some simple messages of loneliness written on the ceiling directly above my head. One read, "Debbie, I love you."

The phrase that struck me the most was, "...this man-made hell." It leaped out at me like a spark of illumination. It seemed so true that even today, I consider the psychological component of imprisonment as a kind of hell.

At first, I wanted to add to the legacy. But then a thought entered my head, *"Only fools seek glory in hell."*

We all knew when someone arrived in the Box, even if we were asleep. The opening of a cell door was always accompanied by a multitude of loud, erratic footsteps that generated a mixture of fear and anger. The Doom Squad always got a kick out of trying to make you beg, scream, or yell in pain, and on some occasions, they would return for additional recreation.

Doing time in the Box had a way of making even your enemy a friend. Some of us were forced to come together in those times of crisis.

As my time in the county jail dragged on, I would learn that most of the other inmates were not assassinating my character or secretly scheming to jump me. Just a key handful were.

One of them was a guy named Donald Crump. He moved to the same tier as me, in a cage right next to me. I didn't know he was the person I almost had a fight with at an earlier party at the same house, just one week before Sherese's death. Nor did I know he was one of the guys Sherese allegedly got into a car with on the night she was last seen alive.

But Crump knew exactly who I was.

One night, he was in his cell, loudly talking shit with another person. He was shouting indirect threats. For some reason, I found myself wondering if he was referring to me in his comments. I felt as if he was trying to challenge me.

The next day, he went out of his way to appear friendly.

About a week later, a man from Bellport named James Washington came through. He was locked on the other side temporarily and was about to be bailed out. I only had an opportunity to talk with him once through the gates at the back of the tier. He told me he had been at the party and what he knew.

He didn't tell me he would later be a witness for the prosecution.

He told me the names of the guys in the red car. When he mentioned Crump's name, I was shocked. The fact that one of the individuals who might have killed Sherese was locked in a cage right next to me enraged me.

I knew I should wait for the right opportunity but became impatient.

Fuck it, I decided that same night. *I'm getting his ass in the morning.*

I knew Crump had a few homeboys on the tier who would back him up. This would leave me very little time to do what I wanted to do.

If I get jumped, I thought to myself, *it will have to be in the morning*. That night, I thought about what he'd done to Sherese. I went to sleep thinking about destroying him.

I lay in my cell the next day waiting for the guys who had court to leave and for some of his homeboys to go to the yard. I wanted the tier to thin out as much as possible.

Then I made my move. I ran out of my cell and began beating Crump. I had only one aim in mind. I overwhelmed him with so many punches he instinctively went into submission and started yelling out to some of his friends for help.

Everyone was caught by surprise as I pounded Crump into total submission. A few of Crump's friends finally jumped up and stepped in to break up the fight. Outnumbered, I was forced to retreat. I had never in my life attacked an individual with so much force.

I was ordered to my cell while Crump was taken to the hospital. He hollered he was going to get me back as he passed me.

Crump was moved to another tier and shortly thereafter went home. When they took him out of the gallery, I laid in my bed in a rage, waiting for the Doom Squad.

Crump had an identical twin brother who was also in and out of the county jail around that time. I had no intentions of making sure who was the right one. Besides, I couldn't afford to take the chance of sleeping with either one nearby.

Not long after my incident with Crump, I ran across a guy who was on the tier at the time of the fight. He informed me that a few weeks after the incident, Crump had told him he was going to get me back by testifying against me.

After I told the guy why I did what I did to Crump, he was taken aback. He told me he would testify for me at trial if I needed it. I declined his invitation.

It turned out the guy had been telling the truth about Crump. Out of nowhere, just prior to trial, Crump came forward to testify as a witness for the prosecution.

I moved to a tier and got into yet another encounter, this time with one of the other teens from the red car, Rawlieh Harris (the third was named Larry Monroe). They were waiting to be sent to the Farm, another part of the county jail, to do time. I found out who they were from Harris.

Harris started a conversation with me. Like Crump, I didn't know who Harris was, but he knew exactly who I was. He told me he hung out in Bellport and used to see me walking the streets alone late at night. He put me on the defensive.

He told me his name and the name of his partner. I didn't make the connection at first. Then it suddenly hit me.

This is the guy that was in the red car! I thought to myself. To him, I said, "You fuckin' liar, you don't know me!" I instinctively attacked with a flurry of punches.

He fell back, trying to regain his balance. Those close by looked on in shock. Monroe and a few of his homeboys rushed to where we were, while a few of the other guys also stepped in on my side, as if to imply I was not alone.

Someone yelled, "Chill, the guard is coming around." We broke apart and maintained our distance, as it was time to lock in.

That night, I laid in the cage thinking I better make my move quickly because it was on. I didn't care that I was outnumbered.

In my mind, I had finally found those responsible for killing Sherese and destroying my life. I wanted revenge.

My thinking may have been discombobulated. But revenge was the only thing that made sense to me. I went to sleep feeling perturbed but ready. Constant contemplation disturbed my sleep.

I never got the chance. The next day, Harris and Monroe were on their way to the county farm for a one-year sentence for a conviction they both just pled guilty to.

I didn't see them again until the trial. They both testified for the prosecution.

Life in county jail, as with any social environment, defines itself by its own codes. I didn't create the codes. I had not yet reached a level of awareness that would allow me to function outside that social structure. Instead, I did my best to survive within it.

Miraculously, I never got hurt or jumped in my county jail encounters. But adaptation forced some changes in me. I discovered new things about myself, as I was determined to survive.

Not all my time in the county jail involved violence. I met some individuals with constructive aims. In the evening, we went to the back of the gallery to reminisce and exchange insights concerning street life and future endeavors.

Most discussions about criminal activities were overly glorified. The conversations were dominated by joys achieved at the expense of someone else's suffering.

Some of it was crazy. I could never see myself committing the type of crimes most of these guys bragged about. I didn't make a correlation back then with my recent feelings of revenge. I certainly was not in any position to judge. Nevertheless, most of these young men would return to the outside world with an opportunity to fulfill their objectives while I remained locked up. I had mixed feelings about seeing someone go home. I was glad for them but knew in my heart I should have been the one leaving. Most of them would be returning within months anyway.

Women were a perennial topic in the county jail. My lack of experience in this area limited my discussion, leaving my conversations more theoretical than real. I'd had very few relationships or sexual experiences. I was a late bloomer.

My interest in girls had only begun to blossom just prior to my incarceration. I never fully understood the importance of intimacy until then. That was when both loneliness and my hormones went into overdrive.

There was something special about receiving letters in the county jail. It was an excellent avenue of escape, an intimate form of expression. Establishing relationships through the written word could penetrate the introverted walls of my wounded psyche. It also served as another set of eyes to the outside world.

I will never forget my first correspondence. For the first time in my life, I found myself revealing what I was going through. Correspondence helped me to get in touch with my own strengths and weaknesses. It enabled me to release some of my frustration and unveil some of my deepest feelings.

I hadn't imagined that such strong relationships could be built through corresponding. Over time I would learn that people can play a significant role in other people's lives through a consistent exchange of words. Powerful human emotions ride on words.

Many of the initial letters I received were blessings from friends. They wrote in support of my innocence. Some of these friends wanted to let me know I was loved; they were in my corner. It was healing to know how they felt.

I was aware that this nightmare had had a profound effect on them. Most of their parents tried to stop their daughters from corresponding with me. In a few situations, we were persistent and continued to do so, at least for a while, by using other means.

A lot of the support in the community came from my own age group, especially among friends and associates who knew both Sherese and me. Most of the support from the adults came from those who knew me personally. Not everyone in Bellport supported me, of course; some didn't believe in my innocence.

I felt fortunate when a female I met from Bridgeport stepped into my life. She came to my defense upon hearing the news of my arrest. She knew if I had been the type of person depicted in this crime, it would have happened to her. She would become my girlfriend in a relationship primarily cultivated through correspondence.

For the first ten years of my incarceration, I reunited with a friend and fell deeply in love—until the reality of my predicament caught up to us. After my conviction, I assumed our relationship would soon end. Instead, it only brought us closer together. She was trying to live off slim hope.

It was silly of me to expect someone so young to be willing to commit to over twenty years at a time in her life when I could not guarantee my return nor holistically fulfill a healthy intimate relationship.

Eventually, I knew it was time to free her. She needed to construct a normal life for herself. And I needed to find a way back home. The experience taught me a great lesson: there is no loyalty stronger than a commitment made to an incarcerated person.

During my county jail days, most of the defendants studied the teachings of Islam. The religion of Islam and the general pursuit of knowledge permeated the New York state prisons and county jails. Listening to these defendants converse about Islam brought back memories of one Mr. Muhammad, who I knew from my hometown of Bridgeport.

Aside from the Christian church, the Nation of Islam was becoming increasingly more visible in the 60s and early 70s in Bridgeport's East End community.

The Muslims were not only aggressive in their recruitment efforts; they owned and operated grocery stores and restaurants. In 1974, when I was turning seventeen, I was totally unaware of the reasons for these social movements, which were at the time one of the primary drivers of the struggle for Human and Civil Rights. I had no knowledge of the times in which I lived.

Brother Muhammad, as he was called, worked on Stratford Avenue, one of Bridgeport's main thoroughfares, selling a newspaper called *Muhammad Speaks*. Just about every time he saw me, he made it his business to approach me and preach his religious faith.

"Little brother, did you know the White man (devil) was put on this Earth to rule you for six thousand years? He was created by a Black scientist named Yakub..."

I didn't want to be disrespectful, so I listened, pretending to be interested. But I had no idea what the hell he was talking about.

When he attempted to sell me a newspaper, I would almost always pretend not to have the money. Mr. Muhammad would persist.

"Now, little brother, you should always have a copy of *Muhammad Speaks*. Do you know who this is?" He would point to Elijah Muhammad, the group's long-time leader. "He is the messenger of Allah. Allah is the real name for God."

He almost always gave me a free paper in exchange for my promise to attend a Muslim service at the mosque. I always agreed but never went.

Still, there was one thing Mr. Muhammad would always emphasize as we departed: the importance of knowledge.

He would leave me with a quote. Or he would deliver a warning lecture of some kind. I didn't understand any of them then and can't remember any now.

Despite the kindness of Mr. Muhammad, I was simply too blind to make sense of what he was trying to convey. It wasn't until my incarceration that the seeds of Mr. Muhammad's message to seek knowledge began growing inside of me. Seeking knowledge in the county jail made it easier to relate. It was like reading a book for the second time.

Most African American men in the county jail were embracing the teachings of Islam at that time. They memorized and recited their lessons with pride and walked with the aura of wise men.

The neophytes articulated Islam as the Black man's reality. They discredited Christianity as the White man's religion and Black man's nightmare. That part I could not agree with, having been raised a Christian.

It was not at all difficult to distinguish the fraudsters from the sincere. Some got into the religion and pursuit of knowledge to incorporate wisdom for street game.

Those who were sincere exhibited consistency in their actions. They lived their lives according to the principles they learned or strived greatly to do so.

There were some things I liked about Islam, but I was not about to commit. My heart was still with Christianity, even though my predicament left me questioning faith in general.

One night, I fell into a deep state of depression. I still had problems adjusting and wanted to go home. I started thinking about religious people who kept telling me to pray, that God would answer my prayers. Overwhelmed by emotional swings, I decided to get on my knees and pray.

Before I could get into it, I got up and sat on my bed as confused as I was before I started to pray.

Something didn't feel right. My mind was all over the place.

I started thinking, *God knows I am innocent. Why would God let something like this happen to me? Why hadn't God helped Sherese?*

I was having too many problems trying to accept the fact that God would let something like this happen to the both of us. If God didn't intervene to prevent all of this, why would the Creator help now? Why would he care?

My mind drifted to a few arguments I'd overheard during family gatherings about the pros and cons of God. The major position of those opposing the existence of God was why did God allow so many Black people to suffer during slavery.

Why did he let so-and-so die? Why, why, why?

Then, of course, there were the justifications for the existence of God, such as that suffering guarantees us a place in heaven, etc. With all these things running through my head, the contradictions sent me to bed that night still depressed and confused.

The next day, I woke up feeling a lot better. But those confused feelings I had about God the night before lingered for some years. I held on to my faith, but as more of a tradition. During that time in my life, I had surrendered my will to powerlessness, fear, embarrassment, and hurt that would eventually evolve into hatred, rage, and revenge.

My mind had been deeply damaged by the tribulations of what was done to me. This ticket of suffering I would never willingly purchase, not even in exchange for a guaranteed entrance into heaven. The memories, now an essential part of me, had scarred my mind forever.

In addition to my physical arrest, my mind and spirit had also been arrested. I would remain caged in this triple state of confinement until I was able to make sense of and truly ground myself in spirituality.

I started this difficult journey as a lost soul with no idea how I was to find my way back home. My impetus for knowledge and the need to grow became the driving force that would place me back on a spiritual path and reawaken my determination to persevere.

As my time in the county jail approached the one-year mark, seeing other guys leaving and returning made me feel like an old-timer.

At this stage of my imprisonment, I was not developed enough to effectively cope with and understand the effects this pain would cause me. I coped as best as possible. Breaking down was not an option. A determination was slowly growing within me. It would grant me the power to withstand a system that did everything to assassinate my character and place my life in jeopardy.

If you didn't know me or the facts of this case, you too might believe I was someone who deserved to die in prison. But I should never have been sent there.

I went through difficult periods trying to come to terms with the effects my incarceration was having on my parents and siblings. I could only imagine what they were experiencing. I knew they had been traumatized by the impact of this incident and the systematic attacks on me. I also knew there were a lot of people from my community and extended family who believed I was guilty and didn't support me.

I felt responsible for my immediate family having to live with the shame and pain of my stigma. In the beginning, almost everyone seemed to have difficulty visiting me in the county jail. I could read it on their faces. For that reason, I would refrain from discussing details of my personal experiences and how I really felt.

In 1975, the county jail was set up to maximize psychological torture. There was no physical contact with family. We were only permitted to receive visits in glass booths and observe visitors from a distance or between a divider in the courtroom.

I was in the county jail for approximately eighteen months. Within that time, I only had physical contact with one family member.

One day, I was in the courtroom with my mother and my lawyer. My lawyer must have sensed how badly my mother wanted to embrace me, because he made an open court request to the judge. When my mother hugged me, she started crying and shaking. She didn't want to let me go.

I kept trying to tell her not to worry, that I would be all right and to stop crying. But she couldn't stop. I was feeling an emotional eruption in myself, too. I almost broke down in the courtroom. That was the first time I truly realized the criminal justice system was destroying me and my family.

I couldn't look back when my lawyer took my mother out of the courtroom. I was losing my composure. I grasped what she was going though. Seeing my mother like that deeply wounded me. I wanted badly to make someone pay for her tears. I went back to my cell hurting and flaming with revenge.

I had to be strong in her presence. My strength depended on her, just as her strength depended upon me.

In the late, quiet hours that night, I put my face in a pillow and wept myself to sleep.

My mother is the backbone of my family. She has led and continues to lead with a flexible, rational, and analytical matriarchy equivalent to that of an ancient queen. To experience the abuse of the criminal justice system, including what it subjected my mother and family to, would change my whole way of thinking.

The loving nature I had as a kid was slowly evaporating, and the vapors were fueling disdain within my heart. What would become of me? Would I become another misguided youth, drowning in rage?

I had no knowledge of law, so I placed all my legal decisions in the hands of my attorney. Most of my lawyer visits involved detailed discussions about activities on the night of the party, the names of people I could remember, and other events leading up to my arrest. We also talked about my acquaintance with Sherese and my reputation within the community.

My lawyer and I discussed the witnesses against me, along with the evidence that would be presented in my defense at trial. He talked about legal strategies and my input in decision-making. But my lack of knowledge of law or tactics rendered my opinion moot. Had I known what I know now, I would have been more involved in the process. We would have done some things differently.

One of the decisions my lawyer made was not to use all my alibi witnesses. There were at least twenty people I was with at the party when the crime was committed. They could have accounted for my whereabouts at the time of the murder. I named six of the people I stood around talking with, off and on, for more than an hour before the time of the murder.

Many of them were willing to testify but were not asked.

In addition, the police used scare tactics against witnesses. Some parents wouldn't let their children get involved. Some witnesses gave contradictory accounts of the events.

After fifteen months in the county jail, the time for trial arrived. I saw people from the community come forward and lie in the courtroom. Others gave testimony that helped the prosecution paint a picture that contributed to my conviction. It became one of the most intense events in my life.

The Trial

During jury selection in January 1976, the father of my trial attorney passed away. A mistrial was granted. The trial resumed in March of 1976. Out of a combined pool of approximately 250 jurors, I selected eleven White people and the only Black juror. I was surprised when the Black juror didn't know what a metal afro-pick was. Still, he was the only Black juror, so we felt obligated to add him.

To this day, I believe he was the main juror who held out in favor of acquittal in what turned out to be three-and-a-half days of deliberation. At that time, it was the longest trial deliberation in Suffolk County history.

My lawyer mentioned a plea bargain offered by the court, under the charge of manslaughter in the first degree. He explained that if I was convicted, I would receive a life sentence. Facing a sentence of life in prison didn't really sink in until my trial began.

But my mind was set. Even if I was facing the death penalty, I just couldn't imagine myself standing before my family and community admitting to this terrible act. Nor was I willing to stand before Sherese's family and take the blame for the pain her death had caused them. After what happened to me in the precinct, I promised myself I would die before complying so easily.

My chances for an acquittal were slim. My precinct experience and the fifteen months spent in the county jail had taught me a lot. It felt like I had grown wiser in that period than I had in the seventeen years of my entire prior existence. I had learned the Suffolk County judicial system was discriminatory, unjust, and rotten to the core.

Sherese's mother attended the trial. On a few occasions, our eyes met when we were near each other. I was tortured by the desire to say something to her. For some reason, I just could not bring myself to speak. I wanted to tell her I didn't kill her daughter. It was eating me up inside. I was too afraid of her response. A negative reaction could have been devastating.

When she testified, I found myself identifying with the pain and devastation she was experiencing. It was sad because this woman and her family ended up hating the wrong person. I never had the courage to tell her. I felt like a coward.

The prosecution opened its case by calling John Shirvell, the first detective to arrive at the crime scene. Shirvell described the scene and position of the body. He discussed all the other specifics that take place in the initial stages of processing a murder crime scene.

Shirvell discussed the execution of the search warrant and the demand for an afro metal hair pick before leaving the residence.

The family couldn't find the pick, according to the detective. A family member was called, and a gentleman who approached the home handed a pick to the detective. Shirvell took the pick and left without asking or knowing if the pick he received was in fact the one that belonged to the defendant.

To engender the jurors' sympathy, an excessive number of photos of the deceased was placed into evidence over the defense's objection.

The second witness the prosecution called was Brenda Carlos. Carlos was an important witness because of her close contact with Sherese on the night of the party. Carlos gave two statements to the police, one on the day Sherese's body was found and another two days later.

According to her first statement, Sherese came to Brenda's house about 10:20 p.m. They, along with Brenda's cousin, a younger boy, went to the party. They arrived just before eleven p.m. Brenda didn't know anyone and could only recall two people to whom she was introduced. One was "Kippy" and the other Lee Maynes.

At around 12:45 a.m., Brenda and Sherese went to Sherese's house to eat. Then they returned to the party, arriving about 1:45 a.m. in the morning on January 11, 1975.

In Brenda's statement, given January 12th, she said, "At about 1:45 a.m. I asked Sherese, 'let's go home.' She said no, she didn't want to go home. I said, 'I'll see you tomorrow.' When I left the party, Sherese was still talking to Kippy. I arrived home at 2:05 a.m."

Brenda gave a second statement to the police on January 14th. This statement was taken only to identify Kippy.

According to Brenda, Kippy was me—Keith Bush.

Brenda also mentioned seeing some boys in a red car—a fact that consistently emerged during the investigation.

She shocked the defense when her testimony during the trial diverged significantly. Over the defense's objection, she testified that Sherese told her she was not going home with her because "the defendant [me] was going to walk her home."

We didn't know who encouraged her to change her story. But it was obviously done to target me, since there had been nothing damaging to the defense in either of the statements she gave to police at the time of the murder.

Sharon Holmes, the sister of Maxine Bell, testified next. Holmes said she knew both Sherese and me and observed both of us engaged in conversation at the party. Holmes then alleged she observed Sherese and me walk out the front door together.

Holmes also testified that many people entered and exited the party for various reasons throughout the course of the night. Holmes said she did not know who Sherese left the party with.

The prosecution called four more witnesses: Debra Bulter, James Washington, Massandra Houston, and Donna Revels. The first two had been walking home that night, and the latter two had been standing on corners, both in different locations relative to the crime scene.

These witnesses testified they heard the voices of two people talking, and then what sounded like screams of "help, help," or "help, rape, help," coming from the vicinity where the body was later found. All four witnesses had initially claimed to have heard these voices two days after the body was discovered. They had not reported anything before then.

None of the four witnesses could determine the identity of the voices and could not tell whether the voice(s) were Sherese or me. Revels testified that detectives kept trying to get her to say one of the voices she heard was me.

When detectives interviewed witnesses, they would start off trying to convince them I was guilty, while at the same time attempting to persuade them to implicate me in some way.

Detectives knew if they could get at least one of the witnesses to say the voices they heard were mine it would validate the other three and strike a major blow to the defense.

Donald Crump would finally get his chance to exact revenge at the trial. To the surprise of my attorney, Crump swore in as a prosecution witness. I could tell my lawyer was shocked, because he looked at me and said, "Keith, that's one of the guys from the red car." As Crump walked around the back and passed the side of the defense's table, I felt my body flinch. My mind was racing a million miles a second.

I wanted to attack him right there in the courtroom. But I kept telling myself, *calm down, Keith, calm down*. Eventually, I was able to do so. Crump and I were the only two in the courtroom who knew his real motive for testifying against me. I didn't even tell my lawyer about my encounter with Crump in the county jail.

The only time Crump glanced in my direction was when he made in-court identification. My eyes stayed on him during the whole process. While Crump was in the courtroom lying, we were engaged in our own secret telepathic conversation. We both knew we were at war.

Crump was considered a prime suspect in this case because of his conviction for attempted sexual abuse. He was questioned on January 19th, 1975. Crump couldn't provide any definitive information about Sherese or me at that time. A few weeks prior to trial, out of nowhere, he came forward to give his false testimony against me.

Crump testified that Sherese and I walked out the front door of the party together. This collaborated Holmes's testimony. According to Crump, I never returned to the party. He almost got into a fight with me at the party, so he watched for me throughout the night. He then testified to his other criminal convictions. He mostly robbed stores, to gather ammunition and guns.

Ernest Lucas testified that he observed a metal afro-pick in my back pocket on the night of the party. He stated the afro-pick he observed was a popular and common hair pick everyone in the community used, including Lucas himself.

He also testified that I wore "a short, leather, blue jacket" that enabled him to visibly observe a hair pick in my back pants-pocket.

This would have been impossible, considering the type of jacket everyone—the prosecution and defense (including myself)—all agreed I wore that night. The jacket I wore hung well below my back pants pockets, covering anything that would have been in my back pockets.

Charles Higgins and Robert Robinson said they were the two people who discovered the body in the wooded area on Mead Avenue.

But none of these witnesses compared to Maxine Bell. She was the prosecution's star. Out of a hundred-plus people who attended the party that night, Bell was the only person who said she had seen Sherese and me "walk away from this party together."

On January 13th, 1975, Bell told detectives she attended the party to see friends, arriving at about ten p.m. She mentioned Sherese, Brenda, Jeanette and Georgette Farmer, Chris Foster, and me as the people she saw.

Then Bell said, "After a while, Sherese, Brenda, and Keith came outside, and we were all talking while sitting on a bright red car... Brenda left by herself after asking Sherese if she wanted to go home. Sherese said no."

According to Bell, "Then Sherese started talking to me and Keith out in the street in front of the house of the party. Then Sherese said that she was going home, and I said, 'I'll walk with you,' but she said no, because Keith was going to walk her home. I then started walking a couple of feet ahead of them because Sherese and Keith were hugged up."

"We walked up Bourdios to Hampton Avenue, then made a left, walking westward toward McDonald Avenue," she continued. "I then looked around and saw that Keith and Sherese were not walking behind me. I then yelled back to Sherese, 'I'll call you tomorrow.' I continued to walk to the abandoned house I had been living inside of."

Bell swore under oath that the second statement she gave to detectives on January 14th excluding Brenda Carlos from her first statement was true. Bell then testified in accordance with that second statement that she sat on a car in the driveway throughout the night, talking with Georgette Farmer in the presence of Chris Foster when Sherese and I allegedly came out of the house together.

Next up was Sherri Young, Sherese's mother. She gave her version of events, including her interaction with her daughter on the night of the party. She also talked about the actions she took after her daughter didn't return home that night, as well as events leading up to the time her daughter's body was discovered.

After that came Leslie Manugault, the assistant principle for Bellport Senior High School. I was a student in the 11th grade at the time of the murder. Manugault recalled seeing me on January 14th in a hall talking to two youths who were not enrolled at the high school.

It was obvious the prosecution was attempting to use Manugault to dispute the defense's case that I was not released from school by Stewart. Manugault gave a different recollection of the time and believed I was in my last period and had left school on my own at that time.

According to Manugault, after we told him about Stewart and our willingness to help, he immediately warned us about talking to strangers. He had no knowledge of Stewart coming back up to school to release me before the end of my school period.

Then the prosecution called the two police officers, Robert Horton, and Donald Marques, who had handed me over to detectives for interrogation. Both officers testified they picked me up at Stewart's home and turned me over to detectives for questioning.

Detectives August Stahl and Dennis Rafferty were called to the stand to testify that the self-incriminating statement I had been forced to sign had been voluntary. The bulk of this testimony was placed in the hands of the shrewd, articulated rookie detective Rafferty. Stahl's testimony was collaborative.

Rafferty testified I was a suspect because of Maxine Bell's statement. According to these detectives, I was asked to accompany them to the fifth precinct to review a list of names of people who attended the party. Instead, I was questioned about the inconsistencies between Bell's statement and my own.

I was then taken to the main office at Homicide Squad in Hauppauge to see Bell's statement. According to the detective, after questioning and discussion of Bell's statement at five-fifteen p.m., I said, "I got scared and ran back to the party." Then there was a half hour of continued questioning without answer. At five-forty-five p.m., I allegedly made statements implicating myself.

Rafferty also testified that everyone ate from seven p.m. to seven-twenty p.m. At eight p.m., the confession was produced in writing. I supposedly refused to make a phone call. I was held in the Homicide Squad Lieutenant's office from 4:30 p.m. to eleven p.m., without leaving for any purpose.

The prosecution did not introduce into evidence the black plastic pick found at the crime scene. Instead, they introduced a wooden pick with metal tines. The pick belonged to my cousin— the relative who had been called to my home.

After my arrest, detectives served a search warrant at my house. They refused to leave until they received a metal pick identical to the one I described. There were none at my house, so one of my brothers called my cousin, who came over and gave detectives his pick. It was the most popular style. The same model as my own.

Dr. Howard Adelman, the Deputy Chief Medical Examiner, testified he examined the puncture wounds around the lower area of Sherese's back. The wounds appeared in patterns of two, three, some four and a few in five punctures. The patterns of three were consistent with the tines of the ten-pronged afro-pick he examined.

There was testimony about abrasions on the victim's face and neck that indicated a struggle. Adelman said, "There were bruises, a large abrasion on the chin, multiple scratches on the face, there was swelling on the lips."

Detective Nicholas Severino, a serologist from the Suffolk County Crime Laboratory, also testified. He said that out of the eight fibers he observed in the material removed from beneath the victim's fingernails, three were similar to cloth fibers from the multi-color waistband around the jacket I wore that night. He also found a red and blue unidentified substance.

Severino testified it would be possible for someone to get fibers from the jacket under their fingernails if that person ran their hands across a jacket in a very hard manner. The logical implication was that the victim struggled with me and the material from my jacket lodged under her fingernails.

Severino gave his scientific opinion, over the defense's objection, that the similar cloth fibers between the fingernail scrapings and the jacket were the same.

Severino's testimony concerned my lawyer. He was worried about what kind of influence the detective's opinion would have on the jury. In recess, my attorney asked me if I came into any kind of physical contact with Sherese at the party.

I told him no. The only contact I could remember was when Sherese braided my hair about a week before the party. After she finished, Sherese brushed hair off the same jacket.

During the presentation of the prosecution case, I could not believe what I was hearing. I knew that Maxine Bell (prosecutor key witness), the detectives, and their so-called expert witnesses were flat out lying under oath upon God's name and holy scripture.

The case was then handed over to the defense. Only sixteen witnesses were called. Other alibi witnesses had expressed interest in testifying but were not called. My lawyer had concerns about too much inconsistency in time differences and events, even though the prosecution built their whole case on this same foundation.

Christopher Foster testified that on January 10th, 1975, he went to the party with Larry McMillan, Georgette Farmer, and Malvina Griffin. They arrived in a red and white car. Foster and Farmer got out of the car, walked to the door, back to the car, and left. He did not see Maxine Bell, Sherese Watson, or me.

Georgette Farmer testified that she went to the party with McMillan and Foster. But Farmer never mentioned Malvina Griffin. She said they sat in McMillan's red and white car.

Farmer disputed Bell's testimony, who had testified that she had sat on Foster's car talking to Farmer at the party.

If the second statement Bell made about Sherese and me coming out from the party together had been true, and this conversation Bell had with Sherese had also taken place, at least one other person should have observed this outside. No one said they even saw Bell at the party. That includes Foster and Farmer—the girl Bell said she had been talking to who was in the car.

Lenora Hart was my main alibi witness. She told the court she was on a curfew and her mother was outside around midnight, waiting to pick her up. She asked me if I could talk to her mother to see if she could stay longer, and that her boyfriend, Gary, and Chris Watkins would walk her home. After confirming this with Gary, Hart and I left the party to seek her mother's permission.

Hart also testified that Sherese left the party at approximately one-fifteen a.m. Hart remained in my presence from the time Sherese left until approximately three a.m. She testified I never left the party during that time.

Hart's mother, also named Lenora, testified that she did allow her daughter to remain at the party with me past her curfew. She also said I had agreed to make sure her daughter got home safely.

The elder Hart also talked about the relationship between her family and mine. I was the only one at the party she would allow her daughter to remain with after curfew.

Nora Rush grew emotional during her testimony, saying Sherese came out of the house and got into an all-red car with three Black youths, "none of which was the defendant." She said they drove off together.

When the district attorney tried to attack her on the witness stand, Rush broke down in tears. She stressed seeing Sherese get inside of the red car and leave the party.

Ernest Lucas was a prosecution witness who also testified for the defense. He said that at about midnight he had gone to Hudson's house, and on his return to the party he saw a red car pass him at one-fifteen a.m. with quite a few people in it.

He did not see Sherese or Bell upon his return to the party, but he observed me standing near a wall talking with Hart and Gary Watkins. He added that he went to sleep within twenty minutes and never saw me leave the party.

Cleveland Jackson testified that the party was held at his house. He saw Rawleigh Harris and Donald Crump in the red car. He knew both Crump and Harris.

Charles Corbin's testimony collaborated on the approximate time and events described in my original statement and trial testimony. He acknowledged seeing me at the party, going to my house with me to eat, and returning to the party with me and two other friends. Corbin went home for the night within an hour after that.

Corbin further explained that he and his friends were the only people, other than the police themselves, who were aware of my whereabouts when I was taken to the precinct. He said he and friends went to the precinct four times, and they were told by the police officer at the desk, "No, he had nobody by that name down there."

George Gholson testified that he received a phone call at approximately two a.m. on January 15th, and he went to my home. The detectives were inquiring about an afro pick. He gave detectives his pick, which was an identical model to mine. The detectives never asked him if the pick belonged to me.

Gholson also collaborated Corbin's testimony in that he, his friends, and the police were the only ones aware of my whereabouts. He spoke personally to the police officer at the desk. He was told they had nobody by my name at the precinct.

I testified in my own defense. I gave an in-depth description of my original statement to police on the night of the incident. I described my activities until the time I was taken from school and turned over to the police. I described the horrible experience I had in the hands of detectives from the time I arrived until I was forced to sign a coerced statement and arrested for the crime.

My mother, Lorraine Bush, testified too. She said that police officers came to her house and took items of my clothing and inquired about an afro comb at two a.m. January 15th. They couldn't find my pick and said they wouldn't leave until they got one. A phone call was made to Gholson, who came to the house and gave the police his metal pick. After receiving the pick, they left.

Next came Kevin Brame, who said that I came out of the house where the party was being held with Davis and Scruggs and helped him with his car. After getting the car started, Brame drove me home. He dropped me off around two-thirty a.m. He did not see Sherese at the party.

The contention that the body may have been placed at the scene was a controversial portion of the defense testimony. Three witnesses—Alfonso Belford, Terry Belford, and Lee Maynes—were firm in their testimony that Sherese's body had not been in the area Sunday morning where it was found that same afternoon.

The Belford boys had gone to the vacant lot that morning to play and look for berries. Both kids described a familiar tree stub and area where berries can sometimes be found. They didn't see a body.

Maude Hudson claimed to have been one of the first people at the crime scene. She was there before the first detective arrived. Hudson, a religious woman, claimed God had told her to touch the body. From what she said, it appeared she felt the need to know if the deceased was still alive.

Hudson further testified that when she touched the body, she felt Sherese's fur leather jacket, and it was completely dry—even though it had rained throughout the night and in the early morning of Sunday.

In rebuttal, the prosecution called several detectives who had prepared and helped execute the search warrant. They denied any involvement in assaulting me and alleged that no such thing took place. They corroborated one another's testimonies and acted as if my claim of an assault of any kind was something contrary to everything they represented.

Again, I sat there watching them lie, wondering how I had been so easily indoctrinated into fearing and respecting them as authorities.

Interestingly, none of the detectives claimed to have had any contact with me at any time on the night of my arrest. Obviously, this meant there was no way I could identify any of the detectives as the people involved in assaulting me.

The evidence presented by the defense immediately shifted to the boys in the red car. The prosecution arranged for the testimony of two of these boys: Rawligh Harris and Larry Monroe. They were both granted immunity in exchange for their testimony. They would not be charged for the stolen red car they had on the night of the party. These two inmates were set free for agreeing to dispute the defense's contention that Sherese got into that stolen red car with them.

Their testimonies were similar—they said they stayed at the party for only a few minutes and waited for Donald Crump, then proceeded to leave without him. They testified that they did not know the victim, and that neither she nor any other person entered their car.

The prosecution also called Maybelle Dingle. This witness was provided by Harris and Monroe to serve as an alibi to the latter portion of their testimony in that when they left the party they had gone to another party at Gordon Heights, the next town over.

Dingle said they remained with her at that party before, during, and after the crime allegedly occurred.

The prosecution went one step further to defeat any suggestion that the colored fibers might have originated from material other than my jacket on the night of the party. The prosecution again called Sherese's mother, Sherri Young.

Young testified that her daughter kept her nails closely cut and showered daily. Young said she witnessed her daughter cleaning her fingernails while taking a bath that morning in preparation for school on the day the incident occurred.

I was recalled to the witness stand in surrebuttal. During my initial testimony, I had described some of the detectives involved in attacking me at the precinct. One detective, James Tohill, had distinct features that made him easy to remember and describe.

In rebuttal, Tohill had said he never saw or met me at any time on the night I was assaulted. My lawyer called me to take the stand to prove there was no way I could have identified this detective in detail if his statements were true.

Maynes was also called to testify in rebuttal. According to him, at some point, Sherese's mother asked him if he could gather some friends and check the wooded area. Maynes did so on Saturday.

He testified that even though it rained on and off on Saturday, they still checked several other wooded areas. Maynes, being very familiar with Bellport, described the specific areas he searched on a few occasions a day before the body was discovered.

Maynes emphatically maintained he'd searched that same exact area, on more than one occasion, the day before the deceased's body was found—and the body was not there.

Finally, the prosecution and defense rested.

The Verdict

Now came the jury's time to deliberate. I would have refused another plea bargain if I had been offered one— even if the offer was for less time. The question entered my mind, of course: What if they find me guilty? I would just have to be strong, especially in the presence of my family. I knew I could never allow myself to be put in submission again.

After spending eighteen months in the county jail, the situation had reversed: on the first night of my deliberation, nearly everyone on the tier eagerly waited for me to announce acquittal. Even some of the guards wished me luck. That first night, I laid in bed thinking hard. So many things were going through my head. Eventually the stress won out and put me to sleep.

There were a lot of people in court on my behalf. Everyone was waiting.

There were requests for trial testimony to be read back the second day, but still no verdict. The third day was the same. Some of the other detainees told me it might be a good sign.

My lawyer presented a motion for mistrial. The motion was denied.

The courtroom was packed on the day the verdict came. After three and a half days of torture, the time had arrived.

All eyes were glued on me as I was escorted into the courtroom. There was a silent tension in the air. Then there was sound of shuffling as everyone stood while the judge approached the bench. The jury was called in. The foreman announced they had reached a verdict.

When I looked at the jury, I got a strange feeling. Something didn't seem right. My heart started beating fast. Some of them looked away—maybe indicating they didn't believe in their own decision? I found myself struggling to remain calm and focused. The judge asked that I stand while the verdict was read.

The first count of the indictment, intentional murder, was read. The foreman replied, "Not guilty." My loved ones erupted into loud, joyful cheers. My lawyer turned to the crowd and directed them to be quiet while the second charge was being read. This one was for felony murder in the second degree.

The foreman spoke up.

"Guilty."

An outburst of screams and cries exploded in the courtroom.

As this was happening, the third charge, for attempted sexual abuse, was read. Again, the reply came: "Guilty."

The disturbance escalated. A few of the jury members started to cry. Their task complete, the jury was ordered out of the courtroom.

Simultaneously, a few members of my family jumped up and charged after detective Rafferty who sat in the front row. Other family members just as quickly restrained the aggressive ones. My mother, sisters, and others were in tears.

The situation was getting out of control. I turned around and pleaded with them to calm down. Many of my family and friends were getting too caught up in their emotions.

When I looked at some of them, they looked back at me, waiting for me to give them a sign of approval. They didn't care;

they would have futilely tried to take me out of the courtroom with no consideration for the consequences.

Instead, I pleaded with them to be cool. I was too afraid for my family, particularly the women and girls. I kept my hands up, entreating: "No! No! No! Please, take them out of the courtroom."

My lawyer stood next to me in disbelief. The judge and district attorney looked surprised and fearful. Detective Rafferty ran to the front of the courtroom and was directed to sit at the prosecution table directly in front of me.

After my friends and family were taken out of the courtroom, I turned back around to face the district attorney and detectives. I looked directly at detective Rafferty. I could see the fear in their eyes, and I knew they could see the blood in mine.

My lawyer heard what I was saying to Rafferty and sensed my anger growing. Now it was my lawyer's turn to plead with me to calm down. But I was turning into the sun. Horrible thoughts were running through my mind. I wondered how I could get close enough to Rafferty to attack him before the court officers could pull out their guns.

My anger was cut short by my youngest sister. She came running back into the courtroom, crying, and calling my name. A court officer coolly took her back out of the courtroom. When the officer touched her, I almost lost it. Seligman kept Pleading with me to remain calm.

Seeing my little sister in that state weighed heavily on my mind. I knew she had been traumatized. I would never again be the same because of it. I felt an overwhelming urge for revenge. My life had just been destroyed and my family deeply scarred. As my family and friends were leaving the courthouse, the police and the National Guard arrived in large numbers.

Before I was taken back to the county jail, I spoke with Seligman in the bullpen. He was crying and wanted to approach my family but was unsure of himself.

I told him, "My family knows I am innocent, and they do not want to hear anything from anybody. You must leave them alone until they calm down."

I returned to the county jail hurt, emotionally drained, and extremely disappointed. That night, I laid in my bed thinking about my family and believing I did the right thing.

Even if I wanted to explode or break, I would never have done so at the expense of jeopardizing the safety of my loved ones. Love means never putting someone you care about in harm's way, never leading them into danger for selfish, retaliatory, or out of control emotional responses.

I was so caught up in my devastation that it didn't even occur to me: I was facing the rest of my life in prison.

It was like being knocked down and stomped on. The hardest thing was getting back up, regaining consciousness, and finding a way to recover from this unthinkable blow.

I got very little sleep that night. I kept waking up, not wanting to believe what had just happened. It was almost impossible for me to comprehend. I kept saying to myself, *why me?* I had never done anything to deserve this.

The last thing I remember before falling asleep was wondering: Where is God? Why isn't God here for me? Why wasn't God there for Sherese?

The next morning, I woke up with a completely different perspective. My stay was no longer temporary. Prison was now my permanent hell. The next challenge would be my preparation for sentencing. I had to let my family know how much time I would be facing.

I also had to make sure they would not be in the courtroom during sentencing.

Because of the vicious nature of the crime, I was expecting a maximum of twenty-five years in prison, with no possibility for parole.

How in the hell was I supposed to do twenty-five years inside of a cage?! That would make me forty-two years old (and insane) before I'd be eligible simply for a consideration of release. I kept asking myself, *what in the world did I do in my life to deserve this? Why me?*

On the day of my conviction, the news spread throughout the community. I hadn't realized there were still some people in Bellport who really cared about me. Some of the ones I knew from school and others I was friends with showed their support for me.

But there were many others from the community, even some from my own family, who did not believe me. There were some teens who attended the party who remained silent. Their parents would not allow them to come forward on my behalf. In their hearts, they knew I was innocent.

As things settled down, police and detectives harassed some of my friends and family members. My mother made the correct decision when she moved her family back to Connecticut to live.

Life Imprisonment

I stood in court on June 16th, 1976, emotionless. I watched and listened to the lawyers and judge determine my fate for the unjust verdict rendered against me.

The day of my sentencing had arrived.

The prosecution did recommend a twenty-year minimum sentence instead of twenty-five. The prosecutor said, "I am making this recommendation because of his age and because of the way he conducted himself when the verdict came in. He behaved and took it like a man. But this was a heinous, brutal crime, and I would oppose the setting of no minimum time he must spend in prison."

My lawyer argued for the minimum sentence, saying, "In my own mind I am convinced he didn't do this act. If he did, it was an act of a moment of passion, not a premeditated murder. The parole board should have the power to determine when this young man is ready to reenter society and contribute to it."

I had an opportunity to speak on my own behalf. But what could I say that I had not already said? I felt there wasn't anything I could do to change the verdict.

I was sentenced to twenty years to life for felony murder and four years (to run concurrently) on the attempted sexual abuse charge.

I remained in the county jail for two weeks, then was transferred to Elmira Reception Center, where I was processed as a piece of state property.

The sentencing judge either ignored or failed to speak about the special needs recommendation to guide the state prison system and its parole commission as a criterion for possible future release consideration. The judge was only concerned with cementing the sentence into place. His closing remarks were, "The only real tragedy in this case is that two young lives have been abbreviated."

My claim of innocence was no longer relevant if it ever had been. I was left to develop myself or submit to prison's powerfully negative forces. Those forces have seized the sanity of men much mightier than the boy who was now being sent there to die.

When I really began to understand the power of choice, I embraced the choice I made to survive, to develop myself, and to find my way back home.

The choice was far easier than the effort required to reach the goal. My thirst for knowledge gave me an edge even against these odds. There were times when the thought of giving up entered my mind. But my experience in the precinct and my desire for revenge served as the impetus that propelled me out of that defeatist state.

My lawyer had an opportunity to speak to jurors on the night of the verdict. Some jurors informed him that they believed the confession was coerced. They said they relied solely on Bell to convict me. My attorney also spoke with Sherese's mother immediately after the trial. She told him that she believed the police had captured the wrong person.

The people in my corner were understandably saddened when the news circulated about the amount of time I had been sentenced to serve. A lot of sympathy and guilty feelings manifested themselves.

After my conviction, all types of rumors flew. But it was too late. The damage had been done. At the time, I really didn't care. I was too badly wounded. I felt betrayed by the people in my own community I knew could have helped me.

There were a lot of other people who attended the party—people who knew I was inside the party when the crime occurred. They simply didn't care enough or were too frightened to come forward and tell the truth.

I felt like an animal, shackled, shipped to hell, and condemned to live in a cage for the rest of my life.

Years later, I talked with my mother about some of her experiences at the courthouse. She attended most of my court appearances prior to and throughout my trial. She was also one of the few who attended my sentencing.

My mother told me about a woman affiliated with a crime victim organization in Suffolk County. The lady contacted my mother to offer the group's assistance and agreed to drive my mother back and forth to court.

Prior to trial, my mother was approached by another woman in court who worked in the courthouse. This woman, who was getting ready to retire, went out of her way to get my mother's attention. According to my mother, the woman told her, "I want you to know that your son is innocent and don't never stop believing in him."

My mother replied, "I know my son is innocent."

But the woman went on. "There is something they are doing that is not right, and don't ever stop fighting." My mother asked the woman what she was referring to, but the woman told her she couldn't talk about it. She just insisted we keep fighting.

My family returned home hysterical on the night of my conviction, and soon left for Connecticut. My mother's boyfriend, Norbert, stayed behind in Bellport to watch the house while the others left. The night they left, a woman from the courthouse came looking for my mother. The woman told Norbert it was important that she speak with her.

My mother was devastated by my conviction and eventually moved permanently to Connecticut. She did return for my sentencing, but there was no contacted ever made between this woman and my mother again. It was years later that I found out about the situation. I was able to search out this woman some forty years later. We spoke on the phone in the year 2018. She admitted working for the district attorney who prosecuted this case at the time. But now alleged to have no knowledge of me, the victim, or this case in her response.

My mother was also approached by well-wishers on a few occasions. One lady stopped her to tell her own story. She also wanted my mother to know she should believe me. Her son had been arrested for murder and tried to tell his mother something like what I had. But his mother didn't believe him. She believed what the police were telling her instead.

After the truth came out and she lost her son to imprisonment, she was also living in hell. She wanted my mother to believe what I told her because the police were corrupt beyond imagination.

After my conviction, rumors circulated about at least five other people being possible killers. At that time, most of the evidence pointed towards the red car.

The Year 1976

In June 1976 I was sent to the New York state prison system at Elmira reception center for processing, testing, and orientation. The ride to Elmira was the longest distance I had traveled outside my community at that time. It was incredibly uncomfortable to be traveling such a distance, shackled, handcuffed, and sandwiched between two other prisoners.

When we approached the locking locations, I was taken by surprise. I looked into the interior. I had never seen a set of cages arranged for so many people in one place. It seemed like a mile from the first cell to the last, with four tiers facing each other on both sides.

Prisoners were going crazy as we entered what felt like an ancient gladiatorial arena. The noise traveled like that of a college football game.

As we made our way to our respective cells, all we could hear were rhythmic shouts of "New-jacks, new-jacks, new-jacks!"

One prisoner who arrived with me had long blond hair. As the prisoners noticed, the shouts switched to, "Blondie, blondie, blondie!"

Simultaneously, burning paper bags and other materials were thrown from all tiers.

I could hear some prisoners yelling: "You pretty motherfuckers, I'm gonna fuck you!"

The noise continued for almost five minutes after we were locked in. Then it slowly subsided. The prisoner with the long hair was the main target. He must have been petrified sitting in his cell, forced to listen to other prisoners calling him and threatening out loud to fuck him.

I would later discover this kind of introduction was an Elmira tradition. It was Elmira's warm way of saying "Welcome to Hell."

That night a porter came to my cell with a message from my homeboy, Joe Garcia. He sent me some food and said he'd see me in the morning. Garcia's generosity did little to ease my fears. My concern was not that I wouldn't adjust. I was haunted by the possibility of being in this place for the rest of my life.

Prior to falling asleep that first night, I laid in my cage, thinking. I had to come to terms with this strange world and how best to survive. From my county jail experience and discussions with a few defendants who had already done state time, I had a general idea of what to expect. I knew not to trust anyone, to limit my associations, to always remain alert and never hesitate to attack to protect myself.

It was also clear that, because of the nature of my conviction, I would encounter even greater opposition from a whole new cast of enemies. To make matters worse, there were family and friends of Sherese I would inevitably encounter. Surely, they had developed a greater hatred for me than those I'd encountered in the county jail.

If any of her family/friends ended up in prison, I would have no way of knowing them. It was like living the life of a blind man at the mercy of the unseen. My thoughts were crisscrossed with images of prisoners at the gate bragging about their crimes and other crimes they'd committed but didn't get caught for. These things bombarded my mind as I entered the dream state.

It was rare in 1976 for a teenager to be sentenced to life in prison. During my stay at the reception center, the few of us doing life terms constantly generated discussions. Most lifers projected a persona of fearlessness—sometimes quietly, sometimes loudly. Some displayed a ridiculous pride in their predicament. It was a self-defense mechanism.

Lifers were struggling with deep uncertainty. Most non-lifers were unable to see through this false pride. Sadly, some prisoners looked up to and praised the idea of another individual serving that much time.

But not everyone. Being around someone doing a life sentence can ease the pain of another prisoner struggling with a lighter sentence of five or ten years. By comparison, non-lifers can cultivate some hope in the knowledge they'll ultimately become free. For some prisoners, lifers drive home the importance of eradicating crime from their lives.

Still, there has always been a class of prisoners who see the world only through a criminal lens. They don't realize they're recidivists, trapping themselves behind bars for life. Doing time around lifers does little to deter them.

The influence of criminality, glorified and promoted in our society, has imposed itself upon those held under its grip. Only through personal growth over many years would I come to understand the deeper nature of this force.

Even today, there is a difference between inmates imprisoned for the first time and those who recidivate—who return to prison after being released. Most recidivists exhibit a higher level of awareness. They can make an easier transition because of their ability to readjust to prison life. The biggest problem these inmates have is deep within their being, as the cycle of reimprisonment begins to dissolve them at the core.

The truth is that most prisoners are actors in the story of their lives, as opposed to producers or directors.

Some do eventually transform themselves and go on to be successful. They become directors by building strong foundations and support systems. Those prisoners who didn't make the necessary changes often returned to prison with more time than their first conviction sentence. If they didn't win themselves a life sentence, they may be murdered because of the high probabilities of a criminal lifestyle.

The cycle is real. Even the innocent can be drawn into it and be consumed once they've been put on that treadmill.

One experience imprinted itself upon me at the Elmira reception center. It was one of the major concerns of older prisoners with legally inclined minds who petitioned through administrative means. We were all placed on a mandatory call-out to the law library upon our arrival. These older prisoners separated us by the seriousness of our convictions and drilled us about what we were up against.

We were briefly educated in the law and the importance of the appeal process. We were instructed to submit another copy of a Notice of Appeal to the Appellate Division, even though we had been told by our attorneys that they would be doing so on our behalf. We were not only instructed about the importance of knowing the law but how it should be used as a tool for prison survival and for challenging our convictions.

These intelligent, articulate individuals emphasized the need to learn the law instead of depending solely on an attorney. They were preparing us for the day when we would be left to fend for ourselves without legal representation in the courts.

A lot of the information I gleaned from these educators validated what my trial attorney discussed with me after my conviction. He looked at me sympathetically and told me to study law and keep fighting when I got upstate.

He told me there were some prisoners upstate who are better lawyers than some of the lawyers in the courtroom. He advised me to learn all I could from them.

What was most significant to me at the time, though, was the concern these older prisoners expressed for the younger inmates.

I remember leaving the law library motivated, determined to learn all I could about law. I knew it would be a daunting challenge because of my difficulties comprehending law. It was obvious I needed to do something to improve myself before I could take this on. I decided I would attend school at the facility I was destined for after completing reception and orientation and promised myself I would stay on top of my legal situation.

Anyone who has had a deeply traumatic experience will understand the different stresses and mood swings associated with it. The effects can result in violence, insanity, loneliness, rage, poor health, suicide, and other debilitating conditions.

Mired in this misery, one is constantly challenged to restore, protect, and maintain some sense of sanity. This is especially true in an abnormal environment—even one that has recreational activities and other superficial outlets designed to diffuse tension.

Maintaining my sanity was one of my most important challenges, equal only to my persistence for over four decades to achieve my release from slavery.

There were times when I would find myself replaying the events surrounding my predicament. It regularly ignited a flare of internal rage that fueled itself in the hatred I was developing for those I held responsible for my suffering.

At that time, I didn't realize how the desire for revenge was slowly eating away at my humanity. Being held hostage by this deep-seated anger, internalizing this poisonous energy, had made me feel like an atomic warhead wanting to explode. It was like living on the edge of no return.

Never had I experienced so much hurt and hatred. It was pushing me toward self-destruction. I was making myself a victim of my own pain at the same time as I was being bound to circumstances, I didn't have the capacity to change.

I was confined in two worlds: one in a plantation type prison life and one in a psychological abyss. The oppression was slowly eating away at my sanity. For many years, I festered in this constant malaise. In time, I came to the realization that if I was to maintain my sanity, I would have to learn how my mind works, so I turned my attention to the mental world. I had no more trust in belief systems or the government and its institutions that felt they had the right to define, dictate, or control me.

As I began to open my mind to my own mental world, I experienced an even deeper sympathy mixed with sorrow for

Sherese and what was done to her. Many times, I found myself wistfully thinking about what I could have done to save her. Why couldn't I see it coming? This kind of thinking left me frustrated, upset, and confused.

From the time of this incident to the present I only had two dreams involving Sherese. One weeks after I arrived at Elmira's reception center. The dream was vivid. Sherese and I were the only people in it. She was walking up Bourdios Avenue toward Hampton Avenue, the same direction fabricated in the prosecution's key testimony from Maxine Bell. From a short distance behind her, I trotted to catch up while yelling out her name. Sherese ignored me and increased her pace. I caught up anyway. As I approached, I slowed and called her name again.

She just kept walking.

In the dream, I put one hand on Sherese's shoulder to stop her from walking, thinking she would turn around to face me. In that instant, her body transformed into a mirror-shaped image in the sky just above me.

In the middle of the round image, her face appeared, supported by a frame in a glassy circle. She looked down at me with tears in her eyes. She was crying and shaking her head from side to side, as if to say "No, no, no."

I stared upward and pleaded with her. "Sherese, tell me, who killed you? Please tell me who killed you. Please!"

She continued crying and shaking her head, while I continued to plead with her.

Just as it seemed she was about to say something, the image rose into space. She looked down upon me as she ascended and continued to cry. I yelled her name.

Simultaneously, I woke up.

I laid in my bed trying to make sense of the dream. There was something about it that seemed so real. For many years, the dream kept surfacing in my mind, even though I was at a loss for what it meant. I kept straddling two contradictory interpretations. It seemed Sherese was upset about something or what happened to her. But my second impression was that she was afraid for me. It made me feel she was trying to warn me about something.

If someone wanted to kill me, how would I know? Sherese certainly had family and homeboys I didn't know about. They were mixed in with hundreds of other prisoners running wild in an already violent setting.

I would only have one other dream about Sherese during my many years of incarceration. The second dream occurred three years after the first. It was short but just as vivid.

I found myself transported to the house party. I was again following Sherese from behind, pleading with her to tell me who killed her.

She walked through the door into the party and directly through the living room. I continued following her and asking her the same tired question. I persisted, but it was like she couldn't hear me. I woke up without getting a response.

I pondered over that dream the next day, searching for an answer to allay my confusion. As far as I knew, the three boys from the stolen red car killed Sherese. I just couldn't understand why I was so persistent in asking the same question about who had done this to her.

Approximately two weeks after the second dream, another strange thing happened. One night, I was awoken from my sleep by someone calling my name out loud. "Keith!"

As I awoke, I heard myself responding, "Huh?"

It took me about five seconds to focus my attention back on reality. I started to call out again, wondering if it was someone from another cell who had spoken my name. I sat there for a moment, puzzled, and listened for a second call, then wondered if I had been dreaming. I got up, walked to the cell bars, and looked out. It was late. All the lights around me were out. I got back in bed, questioning if it had been my imagination. I laid there thinking about it until I eventually fell back to sleep.

My two dreams about Sherese may not seem like much, but they did help to fine-tune my awareness for what was about to come. The suggestion that I might be in danger would become truth.

Those were the only two dreams I ever had about her. One of the dreams was enough to reveal, in time, more than what it appeared to convey. That latter dream may have been hinting at a different story than what I knew at the time and raised new questions about who else might have committed the crime.

Preparing for the Unknown

One month into my stay at the reception center, a third-party message was sent to me from Elmira's general population. A Long Island homeboy sent a warning to me that there might be trouble if I was sent to the general population.

The only thing left was to wait until my time in reception was over to see where I would be sent. When that time came, it turned out to be the last place I wanted to hear.

My cell door opened abruptly. The prison guard shouted, "Pack up, you are going to general population."

I was on my way to Elmira's general population to confront another round of opposition. Why should I have assumed transferring to another prison would have been any different? Wherever I went, it was almost certain I would clash with somebody about the crime for which I had been convicted.

The day I moved to Elmira's population, I was tense but alert and ready. I was looking for a way out of prison, not a way to increase the time I was already doing. A major confrontation was the last thing I needed.

But I wasn't a fool. I knew what I needed to protect myself—or at least easy access to one. One of my homeboys took care of me and assured me I was not alone.

In those days, the Long Island population was one of the smallest groups in the New York state prison system. Although we were outnumbered, a core percentage of us was unified and understood how important it was to stand together. We were always the outnumbered warriors but were referred to by some with the Long Island banner, "Strong Island."

The prison codes and its lifestyles were a little different from those in county jail. Adjusting to the demands prison placed on you was the best way to ensure your chances of survival.

My first observation about Elmira's population regarded the way in which social interactions among prisoners were more pronounced than those allowed at the reception center. A lot of prisoners grouped together according to the geographic communities they came from, religious affiliation, or ethnic identity.

I merged with a core group of the Long Island crew.

The state prisons are different. The arena is much larger than that in the county jails. The number of competitors increases, and so do violent incidents. Although respect is the golden rule in prison, there will always be someone eager to test you.

And even if you're as entrenched as possible, there will always be someone around you—someone you may not even suspect—capable of dethroning you. Your reputation increases with victories but decreases just as swiftly with defeats. Even the so-called toughest, who pursue confrontation and war, eventually taste their own blood.

Prison codes in those days were far more deeply ingrained than the codes that define normal community life on the outside. Prison codes emphasize the importance of being fearless, fierce, and ready to act.

Still, that can lead to incredibly dangerous consequences.

Since we are always accountable for our decisions, bad choices could lead to a longer prison stay. Good choices offered the reward of safely making it through another day.

Some prisoners make crime their careers. I met some doing prison bids for a second or third time who had a troubled past that went back to their juvenile years. They developed a lifestyle that was tailor-made for prison life and understood the inner workings of the prison world.

Many of these prisoners were intelligent and articulate, but in a strange way. They were more influenced by crime and prison culture than by the often-rational words they expressed. Many didn't seem to care that they were undermining their potential and wasting the gift of life. I was more impressed with their ability to communicate than I was with the things they bragged about in war stories of a harsh life of crime.

Although some of these prisoners were on a different trajectory from me, I learned a lot from them. I was introduced to some excellent information, which became an important stepping-stone in my development.

I attended school for half of the day at Elmira. The other half I devoted to acquiring a vocation. I spent some of my leisure time in the law library trying to understand the law.

This was an extraordinarily frustrating time in my incarceration. I had no idea what the law books were trying to tell me. Each time I went to the law library, I left irritated and drained.

It was difficult having to face the fact that I couldn't help myself no matter how much I wanted to. But I didn't know what to do other than to keep trying, and I would inevitably return to the law library for another try.

Why should my ignorance add to my despair? Ignorance has never produced success for anyone. Why should I be the one to embrace it?

I had placed myself in an educational environment so that I could strive for the tools I needed to help myself. But instead of making progress, I was only becoming angrier, more frustrated, more impatient, more stressed.

I was relieved when the court assigned an attorney to represent me on appeal, but I was also intimidated. The lawyer was a woman. Being represented by a female made me wonder whether she would be prejudiced against me because of the circumstances of the case.

Because of the difficulties in understanding law, I found myself placing all my confidence in my attorney. This was contrary to what I had been told to do by my trial attorney and the law library clerks at the prison.

Obtaining a lawyer also gave me an opportunity to seek the easy way out of the difficulties that were overwhelming me. Like most prisoners, I was more comfortable seeking solace in time-consuming outlets. It's difficult to do time constructively without an outlet.

Having an outlet is an important way of diluting the seriousness of a dilemma. Outlets can serve as a pressure releaser and even offer some joy. My outlets shielded me from the constant reminder of the harsh existence I was living. They kept me from falling into a deeper state of depression. They provided temporary contentment.

However, outlets have both negative and positive effects. They can be habit forming, leading to addiction. At the beginning of my incarceration, the need to obtain my freedom and to empower myself was sidelined by these distractions.

Basketball was the prime suspect.

It was more important to me to look forward to the next recreational period than to tackle the challenges I'd needed to overcome or master as the best way of dealing with my predicament.

I knew I needed to be more serious about my education. I was doing a disservice to myself, undermining the little chance I had for successfully litigating my release.

There would come a time when I would find myself alone, totally unprepared to continue litigating, when the case fell to me to pursue without legal representation. Exactly as my peers had predicted.

Nineteen-seventy-six was a disaster. The year began with my conviction and life sentence in prison, followed by a murder contract for my life. The year ended with an even greater shock: the death of my father.

Of these heartbreaking disappointments, my father's death affected me the most. The thought of losing a member of my family while in prison hadn't entered my mind.

Losing someone is one of the worst prison nightmares. The death of a loved one is, no matter where you are, hard to deal with. Losing someone special to you is like losing a part of your core. I was profoundly concerned by the understanding I would never see my father again. I spoke to him on the phone on his death bed. His condition had deteriorated to the extent that he could only listen to my last words to him without responding. I told him that I loved him and not to worry about me. I promised him that I would find my way back home.

It hurt knowing he was dying and there was nothing I could do about it. The fact that I would never see him again and having to say goodbye without at least hearing his voice devastated me.

I was unaware how all these disappointments would accumulate and negatively affect both my mind and my body.

As time mounted, the need to be strong would dilute itself and become washed away by the accumulation of so many things that seemed to always go wrong in my life.

The week after my phone call with my father, he passed away. I tried desperately to attend his funeral. But since he died in Connecticut, outside New York, the request was denied. I was angry and hurt all over again.

The death of my father was a difficult challenge. Why did he have to leave me at a time when I needed him the most? It was a crucial period in my young life, when I was urgently searching for ways to establish a mechanism for survival. After his death, I had very little to draw from, except the promise I made when I assured him, I would survive. His death shifted me into high gear.

Over the course of my imprisonment, I lost all my grandparents, some aunts, uncles, and many other relatives and friends. I would miss the birth and early development of my sibling's children and their children. Most of these younger generations I would only get to meet on my fiftieth birthday.

Just before I was transferred to Elmira's general prison population, one of my homeboys was approached by two prisoners who knew him but also knew Sherese and her family. They wanted to know about me. They were obviously interested, curious, and were clearly trying to get a read on me. They were surprised by the respect I had earned from the Long Island crew and my willingness to accept the challenge.

I wasn't concerned with a one-on-one confrontation. But I knew there was little I could do if attacked by a pack. It didn't matter, my mind was made up. I was ready to die in battle before I let anybody run me into protective custody. I wasn't going anywhere.

I had accepted the challenges in the county jail and took this stance with me to the state prison system. Even if it was just a matter of time before I was killed, I wasn't leaving this world for fear of defending myself against any forces that intended to oppose me. I wasn't planning on spending a possible life sentence in protective custody for twenty-three hours a day when I was preparing to fight against a whole system that had no intention of ever freeing me.

When I arrived in the general state prison population, one of my homeboys told me about the conversations with the two prisoners who knew Sherese from "the street."

There were a few conversations between these two guys and one of my homeboys before my arrival. These individuals decided to back off. When I first arrived, I was put on point, even though these two prisoners were locked in a different location at the prison.

It wasn't until years later that I would learn there were a few people secretly plotting my demise. But in this situation, the only thing that stopped them from taking the contract was they wanted more than what was offered. Ten thousand dollars. One of the prisoners contacted the person to tell that individual he thought I was innocent and that since there would be opposition, they wanted more money.

That person never replied.

Years later, I would again cross paths with the person who was offered the contract. He was the one who told me the whole story. He also told me he knew from my homeboys I would never back down. They respected that, but if they had been offered more money, they would have accepted the challenge.

This individual would eventually earn his release from prison, only to return with another life sentence after getting shot by police in a robbery gone bad. His co-defendant extended his life sentence by allegedly killing another prisoner in another prison over a basketball game.

I learned a lot about Sherese before she moved to Long Island from this person. He also told me to be careful, because Sherese had quite a few admirers, and a lot of people were hurt by what was done to her.

In a strange way, we became friends. We used to talk a lot in the law library and in the evening helping each other research and discussing our cases.

Ghosts of Attica

The rapid influx of adolescents entering the prison system in the 1970s led to younger prisoners being transferred to adult maximum facilities. In July 1977, I was one of the adolescents transferred to Eastern Prison.

I accepted an offer from my counselor to transfer largely because Eastern was a lot closer to home. We were one of the first waves of young prisoners sent to this facility. Most of us were slightly under the age of twenty-one.

There is always a minor tension when transferring to another prison. Some prisoners grow closer to one another. Most seek out homeboys or groups that match their current affiliations.

When we entered the general population at Eastern, we were in for a shock. More freedom was allowed at Eastern than had been permitted at Elmira. Eastern was like a wild party. Prisoners hung out in the halls and in cells. There were prisoner-on-prisoner fights and stabbings. Officers and prisoners were also involved in assaulting each other. Prisoners literally ran the facility. There was very little out of bounds.

I was at Eastern for less than two weeks, when a major event went down in the east mess hall. I sat in the west mess hall eating breakfast that morning as two officers rushed through. Prisoners were getting out of their seats and walking out of the mess hall, going in all directions. Herds of officers ran toward the east hall. I was still learning my way around and didn't know which way to go or what to do.

Mike, one of my Puerto Rican homeboys, came around the corner looking for me. He told me that prisoners were taking over the prison. He sent me in the direction of the yard and told me to meet him there, away from the riot, while he went back to participate. Before doing so, he wanted to make sure I wouldn't be lured in. I was led to about twenty-five officers who forced everyone coming their way into the yard. After half an hour went by, I realized Mike had been involved.

Those of us in the yard remained there until approximately ten p.m. We sat, talked, and walked the yard while news reporters in helicopters flew over our heads. It was the first time I heard prisoners discuss the 1971 Attica rebellion.

A few older prisoners who had been involved in the Attica rebellion were deeply concerned about the takeover. Their narrative left us with the impression that a lot of us could possibly die that night. These older prisoners were reliving their nightmares and drawing us into them. They described the slaughter that took place at Attica and the advantage a special task force waiting for the word to kill had over defenseless prisoners.

These soldiers, in riot gear, were now lined up outside the prison. They were waiting for the order to retake the prison—the same way they had at Attica.

Things became more intense when night fell. As the clock continued ticking on what appeared to be a stalemate, tensions ran high, and the patience of the administration ran low. The turning point occurred when most of the prisoners broke into the hospital area. Some allegedly took the drugs there and started to use them.

This led to an internal conflict among them over whether there should be a violent or peaceful resolution. Fortunately, reason prevailed, and prisoners made the decision to surrender. We remained in the yard, heavily guarded, until the prison was finally recaptured.

Officers were lined up on both sides of the long halls leading to every cell block. We were forced to march between them with nothing on but underwear, our clothes in hand. I kept thinking about what I had been told concerning the Attica massacre as I walked gingerly between these officers. *Be careful, Keith,* I thought to myself. An accidental slip would probably have resulted in being stomped on or beaten to death. It made no difference that we were not directly involved.

A lot of the prisoners were transferred to other facilities after this incident, including some prisoners not directly involved in the takeover. I, however, was not transferred.

While at Eastern, I continued my education. I took the GED test and passed it at which time I signed up for pre-college courses before switching over to courses in typing, business law, and management.

This is around the time in my life when me and my family had fallen into difficult times. My mother depleted most of her financial resources trying to win my freedom, and I was left to settle for a court appointed attorney to represent me. I could not afford to miss opportunities to overturn my conviction. All stages of the appeal process were critical.

But it didn't matter. My mother and brothers always came through. My brothers worked and my mother took on a second job.

Coupled with my social security benefits, we used what God provided to help me continue to fight while taking care of my two younger sisters. We rehired my private attorney and was granted a hearing on the issue of Probable Cause.

For someone who entered this strange world so immature and unsophisticated, I was learning fast and adjusting quickly. I studied to develop awareness and expand my comprehension.

I also wanted to equip myself with the ability to express myself with written words. It would be necessary if I was to challenge the injustice inflicted upon me.

In these earlier stages of my incarceration, I was drawn to information on philosophy and books on positive thinking. As an introvert, I found it more effective to learn on my own and preferred to do so in my cell, which was the only place where I could, at times, find a sense of peace. It was like taking off extra baggage; I could be content with surviving another day.

Prison might be the last place most people would think to look for intellectual integrity. Nevertheless, I met some perceptive and inspiring individuals. Some of them chose not to waste their prison time. They studied, wrote information down in the form of lessons, and exchanged ideas within their circle. They exercised their skills at every opportunity.

There were also those who used their intellect to enhance their criminality. They viewed their criminal activities as a profession and took that profession very seriously.

For example, if their crime was robbery, they would spend time in the law library reading and studying cases involving robbery. Their goal was to gain more insight into their trade so that they could become the best at it. They would read books and other relevant materials concerning law enforcement techniques and advances in investigations or tactics. They used their time in prison to educate themselves not only about their so-called profession but also about other related areas. They devoted time to learning business as well, for instance. They believed they could legitimize their wrongdoing, that they could follow the pattern of rich and powerful people who built their wealth through criminal activities.

These prisoners chose to do on a smaller level what wicked men have done in all ages to rule over others. They believed they had the right to enjoy the riches of life with no regard for consequences. If they could not achieve this goal, they were prepared to die trying. They were unlike the average prisoner, who thought small and preyed opportunistically on the powerless.

Despite being power-hungry, some of these ambitious prisoners were also highly intelligent and persistent in developing their craft. Only a few of the ones I knew succeeded. The rest went back into petty crime, fell by the wayside, returned to prison, or got themselves killed.

I met all types of people in the prison system. I even met demons. But the ones that inspired me the most had the best to offer. I was introduced by them to vital writings and had stimulating conversations. I learned a lot of valuable things from these prisoners.

Pseudo-Gods in Black Roles

In August 1980, the New York State Appellate Division, Second Department, held my direct appeal in abeyance and granted me a probable cause hearing based on a 1979 decision from the U.S. Supreme Court known as *Dunaway vs. New York*.

In that decision, the Supreme Court had ruled that in certain cases, a person's confession could not be upheld if the circumstances surrounding his apprehension didn't qualify as a legal arrest. A legal arrest requires probable cause.

The Appellate Division stated, "Where defendant's presence at precinct house was not voluntary and was a result of police deception and trickery, defendant was in fact, 'seized by police officers within contemplation of the Fourth Amendment,' and it was necessary to determine whether officers had probable cause to arrest him at that time and, if not, whether his subsequent confession was fruit of illegal detention."

The interpretation of that decision implied that the way in which I was taken and kept at the precinct station was illegal.

But the judiciary will grant police the right to trick and deceive anyone into their custody if it is determined there is enough evidence to make an arrest. It doesn't matter if the manipulation involves a youth with no criminal involvement and/or with intelligence considered "well below normal." It doesn't matter if that person would need a parent or an attorney to serve as counsel to advise in such an intense circumstance.

Trickery and deception had found a place in the justice system—or so said the high court. The mental state or the age of the appellate did not matter.

Given the sanction to use these tactics, it's no wonder the courts would turn a blind eye to coercion, especially at a time when there was no videotaping of interrogations.

It was not the ideal decision, but I couldn't complain. The higher courts wouldn't even touch cases of this nature. That fact alone made me optimistic.

While at the county jail awaiting the hearing, I was informed of some even better news. The prosecution's star witness, Maxine Bell, had recanted her trial testimony!

The prosecution sent her a round-trip plane ticket from Alabama, where she was now living, to New York to testify against me at the hearing.

Everyone was in for a big surprise when she confessed to lying at trial.

Bell would have been the centerpiece of the probable cause debate. But that debate was watered down because her recantation was now considered exculpatory evidence favorable to the defense.

The prosecution had an obligation to turn the information over to us. We were prepared to argue that even with her prior testimony, the police wouldn't have had enough evidence to justify my detention.

When I first heard about the recant, I was delighted. In my mind, all I could see was my freedom and the impending end of this bad dream.

At the probable cause hearing, Bell approached the witness stand, where she described a completely different version of events from what she had detailed at trial. She deliberately avoided eye contact with me, as if she was too ashamed to acknowledge my presence.

Bell had been fifteen years old in January 1975. She testified that when police took her to the precinct for questioning, she became intimidated and afraid, so she made up her original story and signed the statement in exchange for being allowed to go home. On the day of my interrogation, she was picked up again and signed an addendum.

Bell discussed, in part, some of her reasons for recanting. According to her, she had been at home after the trial, crying and thinking about what she had done. It bothered her. She had been pregnant during trial. Her baby died just a few months after he was born.

In her mind, God took her baby as punishment for what she had done to me. Eventually, Bell went to see two psychiatrists. She remained under psychiatric care and had attempted to commit suicide.

She hadn't told anyone except her husband about her decision to recant. Bell's husband tried to discourage her from going back and recanting her testimony. He even threatened to divorce her if she recanted. Nevertheless, Bell followed her conscience. Her husband, true to his word, divorced her.

Prior to the probable cause hearing, Bell was threatened with being charged with perjury. Her only reply was that she didn't care. She was unable to live with the burden anymore.

As I watched Bell and listened to her testimony, it was obvious she was suffering, seeking a way to free herself from her own pain. She too was trapped in her own version of this nightmare. Yet she had also mustered up enough courage to come forward and finally tell the truth.

The other witnesses, except for Bell's sister, Sharon Holmes, said substantially the same things at the hearing that they had at trial.

Holmes seemed uncertain about what she had said at trial. The prosecution had to pin her down with constant references to her trial testimony in order to get her to comply. When she left the witness stand, she didn't seem content with her own testimony. It also left me with the feeling, had my attorney pressed hard enough, maybe she too would have told the truth.

I was sent back to Eastern Prison after the hearing to wait for a decision from the Suffolk County Court. When I arrived at Eastern, I still felt confident about my chances for winning a new trial. Though, even if I didn't receive a fair decision in the county court, my direct appeal was also pending.

But just two weeks after returning to Eastern, I was transferred to Comstock Prison.

I was not involved in any disciplinary actions and had no idea why I had been transferred to Comstock. In my initial interview with the counselor at Comstock, I was informed that Sherese had a family member working at Eastern as a correction officer.

I was at Comstock for approximately one month when I received a decision from the Suffolk County Court. Judge Tanenbaum denied the probable cause hearing and reported the court's findings to the Appellate Division. The Appellate Division agreed with the findings of the county court and unanimously affirmed it without opinion. On March 11, 1982, the Court of Appeals denied my request to appeal to New York state's highest court.

I was back in my original position.

That same week, I received a letter from my attorney, who was now representing me on direct appeal. He expressed his sympathy and wished me good luck in my future battles. I had cost my family thousands of dollars again, with nothing to show for it.

I still could not understand why all of this was happening to me. It felt like somebody had spit in my face. It felt like I had been told, "As long as it is up to us, you will die in there!"

My experience in the state court system killed any optimism I had for obtaining justice. Years later, when I decided to enter the federal courts, I simply went through the motions. I didn't expect anything except prejudice. And that's all I ever received.

I completely lost any confidence I'd had in the judicial process. I considered the criminal justice system responsible for my oppression. They were in control, the ones making all the disappointing decisions regarding my life.

The appeals process taught me how risky it was to depend on lawyers to do what I should have been helping them to do or doing myself. My direct appeal was over. I had become what the prisoners at Elmira's law library warned me not to become: a prisoner left to fend for himself.

My only options were to submit or step up and continue the fight. I had to stop robbing my family's finances for lawyers who could guarantee nothing. I knew the primary reason for the consistent denials was the nature of the crime.

After I lost my direct appeal, I tried to seek out the most experienced inmate law clerks for their guidance.

I failed to use my time wisely at the beginning of my incarceration. Had I made the proper investments at that time, I would have been prepared to proceed pro se, on my own, to challenge my legal issues at the federal level.

I should have been more persistent in dealing with my frustration when I was first introduced to the opportunity to learn the law.

Although I was disappointed with the judicial process, I knew I had to keep fighting.

I would delve back into my case. I completed a course in legal research and started to utilize my time more wisely in the law library, searching for ways to overturn my conviction.

I had been so pessimistic about the courts' consistent denials that I never bothered to submit a federal habeas corpus application after being turned down by New York state's highest courts.

Instead, I returned to the county court to re-argue the recantation issue. The motion and my request for an evidentiary hearing were denied. I appealed to New York state's highest courts and was again denied.

Nevertheless, the world was slowly beginning to open for me. I was investing in my personal studies and academics, and it was starting to pay off. Things I hadn't known were becoming clearer to me. I was even attracting help from those who would normally turn the other way.

I spent time reading about federal habeas corpus proceedings. I learned that some of my issues in the state appellate court had not been raised from a constitutional angle.

I went back to the state appeals court and give them an opportunity to review the unexhausted claims, or else exclude them from my federal application.

I went back to New York's Court of Appeals for reconsideration, but the motion was again denied. It was clear that the state courts had no intention of rendering me any form of justice. If I was to receive justice, it would have to come at the federal level.

When I finally appealed to the federal court that application was also denied.

Unfortunately, having to learn from trial and error meant exhausting all my pro se denials. This gave the courts the opportunity to slam the doors in my face.

I didn't stop there. I instantly began exploring other alternatives. My next move was executive clemency from the governor. I accumulated hundreds of petitions and attached them to the application. That request was also ultimately denied.

I even sought out legal advice and assistance from several local and national organizations, particularly those serving African American communities.

Still, the results were always the same.

It just wasn't politically correct to take an interest in a conviction as radioactive as mine. Although I continued to persist in seeking outside assistance, I knew I had to stop chasing illusions. I really was on my own.

Developments After Trial

When Frank Turner arrived at Comstock prison, I had just been denied entrance into the Court of Appeals. We discussed the case. To my surprise, I learned he had attended the party the night of Sherese's murder.

He didn't know much about the details of the case. According to Turner, he had been in and out of Bellport during that time, on the run from the police.

He obviously had heard that I'd been arrested for the crime. When we talked, I discovered he knew a lot more than I suspected. He corroborated Nora Rush's testimony, which had placed Sherese in the stolen red car and not with me. He had also seen her get in that car with Crump, Harris, and another person.

Turner didn't know it was the last time Sherese was seen at the party. He was surprised when I told him a lot of people thought it was the boys from that red car who were the ones who had committed the crime. He told me he had just left Rawleigh Harris at Green Haven Correctional Facility in upstate New York.

Turner told me Harris was a Muslim. I immediately guessed why. It was a typical strategy for some people who have enemies or commit devious crimes in the community to convert to one of the many different groups or gangs for protection when they come to prison.

I told Turner the details of the whole incident. He was stunned, and only replied, "Damn, if I knew that, I would have fucked him up."

I asked Turner for an affidavit and permission to submit it in court. He was hesitant. He was the type who preferred instead to address the situation when he got out.

But I pressed him and finally convinced him to do the right thing if not for me than for Sherese. He agreed, out of respect for Sherese and me. I submitted a motion to the county court. Unsurprisingly, the county and higher courts denied my motion for an evidentiary hearing and new trial.

The New York District Attorney's office deliberately withheld vital police reports in my case. One report, dated January 16th, 1975, pertained to information that a male youth, "Poochie Mc They" (spelled phonetically) was alleged to have definite information as to Sherese's murder. "Poochie" supposedly told his mother about the incident. The family had called a lawyer, who advised them to withhold any statement.

If this Poochie had "definite information" about the murder, it would have been more solid than anything they presented against me at trial. The prosecution had an obligation to seek it out and use it against me—unless, of course, it was something that pointed to my innocence. If so, they had an obligation to turn it over to the defense. They never did.

What was that information, and why did a lawyer instruct the family to withhold it if it could have helped to convict me?

In my opinion, the name "Poochie Mc They" could be a code to conceal something they may have discovered about the killer(s) in this case. To this day, I have not been able to find one person who knows who it might be.

There was another report concerning Mrs. Doris Farmer, who contacted police on January 28th, 1975, about threatening telephone calls that her daughter, Georgette Farmer, and another girl, Melvina Griffin, were receiving.

The threats involved a male voice saying, "You be next." Doris had approached her daughter about reporting the calls to the police, but Georgette had refused.

Georgette Farmer had testified at trial on behalf of the defense. We had no knowledge that any threats had been made on her life. The district attorney apparently knew but didn't raise a single question or make any reference to it during cross examination.

I discovered this report as part of a Freedom of Information Act request, I made to the Suffolk County District Attorney office in October 1989. At that time, I was still unable to put the pieces together.

I needed to know: who made the threats, and what did these girls really know that would lead someone to threaten their lives? If the district attorney's office had withheld this information, what other vital information, if any, were they hiding?

Special Housing Unit

The horrors associated with the famous Attica rebellion of 1971 left a powerfully intimidating aura that lingered throughout the institution. Prisoners took forty-two hostages and demanded more political rights and better living conditions. Then-governor David Rockefeller ordered state troopers to storm the prison. Although the rebels had requested peaceful negotiations, these troopers indiscriminately carried out a bloody massacre to retake the prison. In the end, forty-three people were killed: thirty-three prisoners and ten officers or civilian employees. Far more were wounded.

These lost souls thickened the air of the prison with the residue of hostility ever after. Relationships between prisoners and officers appeared to be forever defined by this permanent bloodstain.

Like other prisoners, I felt the tension and figured it was just a matter of time before something major went down. It was sad witnessing how some officers committed crimes that were like the crimes for which some prisoners had received long sentences.

Everyone knew their place, at least in A-Block, the most intense part of the facility. Prisoners entering the facility were usually sent to A-Block, where the unemployed and so-called troublemakers were caged.

The blatant abuse of authority and physical assault on prisoners by officers at Attica gave me a distinctive dislike for being confined there. Resentment had become a part of my daily attitude.

Every prison has its own crew of officers who, like crews of prisoners, prey on the powerless. The only difference is that these officers can hide their crimes within Corrections. There are coverups for crimes both minor and major. Officers are rarely exposed, charged, or convicted.

Corrections officers are protected by the same mechanisms as police officers are—their collaborating entities: bias media, politicians, and the criminal justice system itself. The public would be shocked if they knew just how ruthless some correction officers are in carrying out their duties. Some of their ruthless practices continue to be carried out but are hidden from public view to this day.

Major incidents were common at Attica. One day, officers assaulted an older prisoner in the package room. A lot of prisoners were furious and discussed the need to "get busy." The next day at the morning mess hall chow, prisoners left it up to Messiah, the brother of the prisoner assaulted, to make the call.

Some prisoners were so tired of the abuse that they were ready to make another sacrifice.

But Messiah, who had been put on the spot, was indecisive, not quite knowing what he wanted to do. He eventually wisely opted to wait until he found out if his brother was all right.

The administration sensed the tension. When Messiah returned to his cell, he was immediately locked up for investigation. He stayed locked up long enough to think through the process.

In the time Messiah was locked up, the number of prisoners ready for another losing battle had grown to over a hundred. Just before Messiah came out of his cell, he sent a note calling it off.

I wondered why our fears cause us to hesitate long enough to rationalize ourselves out of a confrontation when it relates to those in power who abuse or oppress us. But when it comes to each other, our fears turn into rage and violence.

I took a job in the afternoon and evening mess hall hours. These hours provided me with more leisure time for law library call outs and personal studies. But I hated Attica and wanted out at any cost.

In the latter part of December 1983, I finally got my wish. I was sent to the Special Housing Unit (SHU) along with six other prisoners because of a fight that broke out during working hours in the mess hall.

One prisoner threw hot water on another prisoner and ran inside the officer's station for protection. The officers violently restrained the prisoner who had suffered burns from the hot water. Some of his skin was pulled off in the process.

I was not personally involved in the fight. I got so caught up in the way officers were mishandling the situation that something inside of me exploded. I lost control. The pressure got the best of me.

The burn victim's crew (except for one prisoner) did nothing but watch and follow orders to stand aside. I challenged the friends of the burned prisoner to step up in defense of their friend in front of the officers and their superiors. I committed myself to stand with them. Everyone present must have thought I was crazy.

In that moment, I just didn't care. I'd had it. I had no concern for the consequences.

Rage sent me on a suicide mission.

I was taken to SHU, stripped naked, and placed in an empty cell encased by plexiglass. There were no sheets or blankets in the cell, only a mattress. The window in front of my cell was intentionally left wide open. The lights remained on twenty-four hours a day.

I knew I had put myself in that situation and had no one else to blame. I was prepared to handle whatever repercussions followed.

The first night, I laid in my bed, freezing, while drifting in and out of consciousness. I was trying to stay awake in anticipation of the officers' inevitable assault.

The following day, I was moved to a regular SHU cell, where I remained for about two weeks. Spending two weeks in Attica's SHU was the equivalent of spending two months in the general population. Officers beat prisoners at random. There was action around the clock.

Every other day, there were cries and screams coming from the cells of other prisoners. It was a no-win situation, so we just fought back. Some even threw feces and urine to defend themselves.

In addition to jumping prisoners, the officers occasionally lit the galleries up with tear gas. That's when things got scary!

I was sentenced to three months of solitary confinement and was ordered out of Attica by the superintendent. I was immediately transferred to Wende Correctional Facility near Buffalo, N.Y., along with another prisoner involved in the incident. He had been sent to SHU for running after the prisoner who had thrown the hot water on his friend.

The day we arrived at Wende, an officer came down the stairs shouting, "I heard we got two niggers down here. Let's hang them."

Here we go again, I thought to myself.

We were the only two prisoners confined in this dungeon. We eventually found out that Wende did have a reception center and a cadre of state prisoners. The remainder of the facility was made up of a county jail population.

At the time, the facility was going through a transition. It had formerly been a jail called Erie County Penitentiary. Places like the law library had not been set up. The grievance mechanism, whereby prisoners could file complaints, didn't exist. There wasn't even a shower in the area where we were locked. It was extreme isolation.

Three weeks later, another prisoner was transferred in. He was the prisoner who had been burned. We updated him about the situation. We then discussed a strategic course of action.

I purchased a jailhouse lawyer's manual to further my education and in anticipation for predicaments like this one. It was in my personal property but had been damaged in the transfer along with everything else. It was good enough for the job. I figured that if we could submit a lawsuit, we would be able to get the courts involved and somehow break the isolation.

The other two prisoners had no confidence in the court system. That was understandable. Neither did I, but we needed to establish a link to the outside world.

We had no idea how we were going to get the lawsuit out. We even considered hiding it in the yard when we went out for recreation, hoping that the other prisoners would find it. Ultimately, we did find a way to get it in court.

I had never filed a lawsuit before, but I did have my manual. When I found out that nothing had been set up yet, the first thought I had was *Constitutional violation.*

It wasn't until the superintendent of Wende received his summons from the United States Marshall that the situation completely changed. We no longer had a problem getting our mail out.

To accommodate us, the facility set up a grievance program and started sending us law books. The superintendent walked regularly through SHU, making himself available to address any problems we were having.

He was obviously concerned about the lawsuit and was adjusting in an effort to render the suit moot. Periodically, a sergeant came to my cell to see if I had any other grievances that needed attention. He also attempted to persuade me to drop the lawsuit.

Here, in the law, was another way of fighting. We detected the concerns of the administration. The lawsuit became our way of striking back at them.

The prison officials assumed we were intimately familiar with the law, and their attitudes toward us changed completely. We had outmaneuvered them, and the administration knew it. What they did not know was that if they had only taken my jailhouse lawyer's manual away, we would have been rendered completely ineffective.

In addition to the boredom, restlessness, and loneliness caused by perpetual confinement, SHU provided time for reflection. My confinement in SHU was where I first came to terms with the impact imprisonment was having on me.

Looking back at my life prior to incarceration had left me wondering who I had become. Was this the person I really wanted to be? How was I to overcome the loneliness, hurt, and rage that intoxicated my consciousness and was arresting my humanity?

I had been in prison for almost a decade and was just now seriously considering the pain this horrible experience was producing in me. The anger I was using to handle my ordeal had put me on a collision course with destruction.

This last encounter with prison officials helped me to realize the concerns I needed to address. If I didn't, I would continue to suffer the consequences of out-of-control emotions.

Things were hard for me. I had very little hope. My faith was shattered. My beliefs had washed away, supplanted by powerlessness. Stress had taken the driver's seat in my mind, and it was leading me over a cliff. My diet consisted of an over consumption of frustration. It wrecked my body and was poisoning my soul.

I had lost my direct appeal on the state level and missed my opportunity to enter the federal court. My faith in the justice system was shattered. The slim odds I had of reversing my case filled me with pessimism, and my focus was dim. Imprisonment was eating away at my sanity.

It was only a matter of time before this river of stress would carve its own canyons within me.

I didn't know if it was stress attacking my body and mind, but I do believe it blended with things like my deep-seated fears, confusion, and escalating hatred for all those who had harmed me. It wasn't long before my body caught up to my reeling mind. I wasn't eating as healthfully as I should have been, my sugar consumption was at an all-time high, and I was as inconsistent in my exercise as I was in my meditation and prayer. But I had relegated these crucial things to the sidelines.

During this period of my incarceration, I was pulled so far outside of myself, my body felt like a dark, empty tomb.

At the root of my physical problems, of course, was my mental state. I was riddled with fear, paranoia, anger, rage, and a desire for revenge. This mental turmoil was quicksand, slowly pulling me down.

At times, flames of rage flared through the cracks of my shattered morality. My anger was gaining mastery over the good person I had been. My inner demons were suffocating me.

I fell off my path of pursuing positive thinking and education. I lost sight of my rationality. I was ensconced in daily contemplation as I found myself dramatizing and rehearsing different scenarios of the ultimate confrontation that would define my fate as victory or defeat.

I was possessed with what I considered to be who I was becoming, and my obsession opened a door of deep hatred. I knew it was the devil appealing to me.

Sick call, the facility's medical treatment location, was slowly becoming my regular haunt. I was breaking out in rashes, hives, and ulcers, all of which were new to me. When I was tense or angry, I experienced fluttering in the chest and an irregular heartbeat. These were warning signs that I was on the wrong path.

Was it my turn to die? Death catches up too many prisoners doing long prison sentences before old age does. Dying in prison is a prisoner's greatest fear.

Doing all that you can to care for yourself is the best way to increase your chances of making it through the day, one step closer to freedom. Depending on the prison medical staff to care for you, on the other hand, is not a wise decision. Medical complaints in prison are rarely taken seriously. Sometimes you get lucky and find a nurse and/or doctor who will do their best to help you, but more often you're on your own.

If the medicine doesn't kill you, the stress will. If you're unwilling or untrained to do research about or litigate against inadequate medical attention, the outcome can be dreadful. Being prepared to fight for what you deserve is necessary.

For years, ulcers ate away at the lining of my stomach. In the beginning, I did not question the medicine being given to me, I just took it because it eased the pain. However, one day, I ran across an article in an old copy of *Reader's Digest*. It was about an Australian doctor who claimed to have developed a cure for ulcers. He allegedly gave it to himself to prove his point.

I took the article to sick call one day and told the doctor I wanted to be treated with this method instead of remaining on medication that would not cure me.

They refused to even consider my request, instead prescribing the same old medication. I filed a formal complaint with the inmate grievance committee outlining constitutional violations. I was prepared to take them to court until they resolved the issue.

Eventually, I was treated as I had requested, and I never developed ulcers again.

That incident convinced me that my health could only be determined by what I was doing—or not doing—to help myself. I would have to stop putting my wellbeing fully in the hands of those I felt did not have my best interest at heart.

I had been introduced to some valuable information in the ten years I had thus far spent in prison. But for some reason I was not developing internally. What I thought was personal development had been purely superficial. I still had no real understanding of the true meaning of development. I also fell short in applying the insights I had gained. This was especially true with some of the information I copied, like "The Scrolls."

One of the scrolls read, "Today, I will be master of my emotions." Yet there I was in SHU as a direct result of my emotions running away from me. Why did I ignore useful advice simply because it conflicted with my desire to enact revenge for past traumas? It did not take much to trigger an emotional explosion and overwhelm rational decisions.

As I searched for answers, I came to the realization that there were incidents from my past I had never resolved. Some I had not even properly explored and didn't fully understand. I had never seen the need to revisit them, and as a result, I lived in self-denial. I was not developing. I was merely stockpiling knowledge.

I began to comprehend that development must entail something more: Inner transformation. A resolution of and reconciliation with internal conflicts that blocks the flow of positive thinking and the manifestation of unique human qualities.

I needed to transform. I had to find a way. I had to travel deep within myself to find where these internal conflicts resided.

How strong was this need to transform? I knew there would come a time when I would be tested again.

While at Wende prison, I tried to get to Green Haven. I even wrote to Classification and Movement (who handle transfers) from SHU, requesting an explanation as to why my transfer to Green Haven had been denied.

I was informed I had an enemy at that facility named Rawleigh Harris. To keep us from coming in contact, Harris identified me as his enemy upon entering the state prison system.

When my time was served in SHU, I was transferred to Auburn Correctional Facility, not far from Syracuse in upstate New York. Just before leaving, I vowed I would reach what I considered a level of "true" development.

I was determined to confront all the demons that haunted me in my inner world, and I entered Auburn highly motivated to redirect my life.

I worked temporarily in the bakery, before transferring to the furniture shop. The change in jobs enabled me to accumulate extra funds to purchase books. I also bought adequate winter clothing and other necessities.

Twice a week in the evenings, I devoted my time to the literacy volunteer program to help prisoners learn to read and write. Who would have thought I'd be teaching others something I'd barely been able to do a few years earlier?

Auburn didn't fit well with my need to change, however. Aside from the fact that it was so far from my family, there were more murders and acts of violence at Auburn than at any other prison I had been in.

Most of these incidents were sparked by old beefs, but all of them involved prisoner-on-prisoner violence.

However, I was making progress, and my focus was slowly shifting away from such confrontations. I needed to move on.

After a year at Auburn, I requested a transfer. I didn't bother to select a specific prison. It didn't make a difference if it was closer to my family. It was clear my request for Green Haven would be denied, so I never even considered it as a possibility.

As I waited for the outcome of my transfer, I started reading a lot about Black culture and other subjects. I had the opportunity to read many books, and the material I was consuming was beginning to leave a profound impression on me.

I left Auburn hungry for knowledge and committed to learn all I could—particularly about African and African American culture—at my next place of confinement.

I would remain at my next stop for over a decade. In that time, my life would transform in ways I never could have imagined.

The Allure of Criminal Behavior

It's true that prison is a microcosmic manifestation of the larger society. But prison is also a place where criminals learn to become better criminals and innocent people are drawn into a life of crime. Prison is also where many lost souls find new meaning in their lives.

Prison is the permanent home for many misguided offenders enraptured by their own delusions of thugism. One thing prison is not and will never be is *a place to be glorified*. After spending over a quarter of a century of my life in prison, I can say that with authority.

The glorification of crime and violence has somehow permeated elements of popular culture. Unfortunately, this influence has consumed some of our troubled youth. It has distorted their definition of reality and fueled their desire to associate themselves with choices that lead to prison.

In most cases, crimes carried out by individuals are the results of irresponsible choices and/or unjustified reactions to failing institutions. These reactions generally find expression in those who are uneducated, unskilled, or discriminated against. These individuals are out to acquire the material gains enjoyed by the so-called privileged and hard-working members of society.

Failing institutions can lead to deprived social conditions. They can breed attitudes of social dissatisfaction and a destructive mindset, particularly in poorly educated or unskilled people.

Of course, the failure of institutions in and of themselves will not lead to crime. But it can enable poor choices, crime among them. And the choice to engage in illegal acts will almost always lead to imprisonment or death.

Aside from attitudes of social dissatisfaction, there exists a much deeper psychological aspect of criminal behavior that accounts for some of the most bizarre criminal acts.

That door is an extremely difficult one to unlock. Mental blockages build up because of past encounters of trauma, abuse, or undetected mental illness. These deep-seated ailments, when unaddressed or uncontrolled, can reveal themselves through aggressive traits. If unmanaged, one act can lead to repetition and habit, a common characteristic in predatory and recidivistic tendencies.

One thing is certain. Even if these incomprehensible acts, to some extent, are influenced by external factors, they cannot be lumped in with the type of criminal acts derived largely from individual greed or socioeconomic dissatisfaction.

Deviant criminal behavior is the exception, not the rule. These types of crimes require their own analysis and unique rehabilitative approach. Whether or not crimes can be categorized is a matter of debate. But what is undisputed is that all acts of criminality are irresponsible and demand accountability.

Prison has become a place where criminal codes are upheld, and criminal behavior acculturated. It's an arena where everyone is tested. Nevertheless, the test is purely mental: only the individual can determine success or failure.

Crime and violence are not actions to be imitated. Remorseful prisoners know this the best. They live with the shame of past misdeeds pressing on them so much that they will do what must be done to become a better person. These are prisoners worthy of acknowledgment for having turned their lives around. They advocate for positive change by example.

Only fools—the weak and misguided—would look to the reputations of others for honor and respect.

Many prisoners live their lives in prison in a state of apathy. Some have become television and recreational junkies who spend their time telling exaggerated (or false) war stories. These types of people salute only the likes of gangster movies and the drumbeat of gangster rap music that praises them for the destruction they left behind. They are blind souls bathing in the limelight of a pretend thugism while secretly stewing in their deepest fears and the pressures that incarceration imposes. The fear is real but rarely mentioned.

Instead, these cultural creations promote the glorification of prisoners as heroes and prison time as a rite of passage.

The saddest part of crime is a criminal's thirst for recognition over the suffering, horrible memories, and sad stories of victimization. The "shout out a praise" by gangster rappers and its social acceptance promoted by movies is designed to appeal only to those who buy into the glory of violence and crime.

Instead of using media outlets to teach the truth, some of these artists and directors sensationalize crime. It's almost as if they're working with the criminal justice system, which must feed off criminal minds to satisfy its multi-billion-dollar appetite.

Most prisoners—the most aggressive in their pursuit of monetary gain—did their deeds at the expense of devastating their own communities. Inside the criminal justice system, they are obediently acting out the life of a slave. In prison, they accept slave wages for mandatory program assignments. They do not fight for fair wages. They would rather exploit families and friends out of billions of dollars (on a national scale) for their own personal satisfactions: catalog purchases, packages, commissary, visitation transportation, visiting high-priced vendors, and on and on.

They passively settle into state prison industries that generate hundreds of millions of dollars annually. They allow the system to rob them and their families out of millions in mandated burdens like court-imposed and disciplinary surcharges.

In the past, some have even used their skills to build prison cells/towers, fixing, cleaning, and serving administrative needs and the communities in the prisons where they reside. What's more, they do this with the knowledge that none of these billions in revenue are used to reimburse their families or to compensate their victims.

The overwhelming majority of prisoners have surrendered their lives to become a prison resource. They do so with the false hope that their complacency, obedience, and refusal to challenge what they know to be unfair policies will earn them early parole.

In truth, many of them spend their time in prison exploiting families and friends for luxury, the same way they exploited their communities before entering confinement. Without prisoners, the criminal justice system could not be the behemoth that it is.

In return for their service, prisoners receive longer sentences, tougher laws, consistent parole denials, no earned incentive allowance (good time), brutality by prison officials (which is rarely prosecuted), mistreatment of families, friends, and volunteers… the list of indignities goes on.

This is obviously not the case for all prisoners. There were those who spent years in the Box for refusing to cut off their dreadlocks for cultural or religious reasons until a court of law allowed the practice. There were many other legal battles fought and won by courageous and intelligent prisoners. They led movements, formed organizations, and created cultural study groups. They changed liabilities into assets. These prisoners returned to their communities with a new mission to raise their children and help develop their neighborhoods.

I know because I was enlightened by some of these teachers along the way. They inspired me to do the same. They did not build up their reputation in prison through violence. They were well-known for their intellect.

Some were fortunate enough to use their aptitude to find their way back home. Others used their brainpower to maintain their sanity after having spent over thirty or forty years behind prison walls.

The Green Haven Experience

Transferring to another facility requires an adjustment. For me, adapting to a different prison environment was not as intense as the trip itself. Traveling outside of prison brings to the surface all the psychological damage caused by prolonged periods of confinement.

The scenery, glimpsed from prison to prison, reinforced the way in which my existence had been denied any chance to flourish. During my travels, I was amazed at the simple pleasure of just watching people driving in cars and walking the streets. I knew they could not relate to what I was feeling.

Transferring to Green Haven gave me even more opportunities to advance my education. My newly discovered interest in African American and African culture led to my immediate enrollment in the Malcolm X Black Studies program. I selected the program that met in the morning hours and utilized my afternoon for law library or recreation.

Black Studies had its own unique struggles. Confrontations between its members and the administration were escalating. The administration had targeted the main instructor, Cardell "Blood" Shaird.

It was alleged that Blood's teaching style and materials were militarizing rather than rehabilitating prisoners. Blood's insights and knowledge were magnetic. Every time he taught; the Black Studies classroom was filled.

Blood and another prisoner named Butch Harvey were best friends. Harvey was another prisoner who made the authorities in the prison system uncomfortable. I was in Comstock when corrections officers later murdered Harvey.

There were prisoners in the state monitored and/or targeted for their abilities to organize and influence. Blood and Harvey were on that list.

He was also bold. Blood attended a class just to debate a professor who published a book that undermined Africa.

Blood intellectually destroyed this professor in front of his students. The man was so humiliated that he grabbed all his belongings and left the prison. That teacher never taught another class at Green Haven again. The superintendent personally banned Blood from the school building. No explanation, no charges, nothing. Blood was no longer permitted in the school building and was not allowed at any time for any reason whatsoever.

The superintendent wanted the program taught by a civilian. But this was a futile effort, as I witnessed the instructors, and their advanced members reduce civilians to students.

When one civilian resigned, he told the education supervisor the prisoners knew more than he did and were better qualified to teach themselves.

I was a cultural neophyte when I enrolled in Black Studies. I read books on the subject, but the books were nothing like the classroom. These men took me on a voyage to places I'd never been.

I had built a foundation on positive thinking but still had not transformed at a deeper level. Black culture provided me with information that fueled my growth toward what I would eventually become, opening doors I did not know existed.

My knowledge extended only to the pictures of Black inferiority painted by institutional racism. This thinking left me, like many African Americans, distorting the question of my identity to preserve my own delusion of who I really was.

In Black Studies, I was given an in-depth introduction to historical events. We learned about other cultures. I was also introduced to the Native American side of my heritage. We covered contemporary issues and current events.

It was the "high science" left behind by the ancients that had the most impact on me—Kemet in particular. I found their teachings interestingly intriguing: Tehuti's hermetic philosophy, astronomy, astrology, numerology, and alchemy.

Reading about the drama of the Kemetic God Heru also inspired me. It did not matter if this story had no basis. What mattered was how I used parts of it for transformational purposes.

In one version of this drama, Heru became the Victorious One. Having defeated all twelve demons in each hour of darkness to become the rising sun. When I achieved my exoneration, I bathed in that emotional surge of vindication.

I knew I needed to reenter that world to defeat my own demons and become whole again. I also realized that Heru was my first visitor, who stopped by to fuel my fire.

I studied hard. Because of that, my confidence and self-esteem expanded. After attending Black Studies for two years, I was removed from the program by the educational supervisor. In that two-year period, I grew tremendously and used my time to build a solid foundation.

After my removal from the Black Studies program, I was determined to stay on the path I had started down. I enrolled in Dutchess Community College in Poughkeepsie, N.Y. for computer data and word processing.

Through hard work and determination, I graduated at the top of my class, received honors and a special plate for most outstanding student.

I went on to earn an associate degree in Liberal Arts at Dutchess Community College, and again graduated in good standing. But institutional education did not naturally suit me. It was too structured and geared toward indoctrination.

I needed to do something, to be active by putting what I was learning to use. I wanted to fight, and Green Haven provided that opportunity. I was drawn to where the brightest of intellects were running their own self-created programs and pro-active movements.

The first organization I got involved in was Project Build, Inc. I signed up for a Tuesday evening communication course ran by its instructor, the Muslim Imam Robert Shaheer. He was masterfully articulate and could connected equally with people inside and outside of his Muslim faith. I was impressed by the way he presented himself as well as the confidence and spontaneity of his character.

I must have also impressed the Project Build's leadership because I was offered a position in the organization. That request was followed up by a letter of invitation to serve on its executive board. I accepted. In time, my activities would include facilitating classes, coordinating family day events, auditorium presentations, group seminars and more.

One of the first things I did was to suggest that Project Build revamp its poetry/writing workshop to create an outlet for the young rappers walking the prison yard spitting lyrics that would remain there. We created a forum for their expression. A battle ground for rappers to compete. Then we put together a show in the prison auditorium, and the general population loved it. This approach was used to bring more of the younger prisoners into the J-school areas where prisoners were conducting classes and workshops.

These rappers were better than most of the rappers signed to labels. Their lyrics were powerful. I would always try to encourage these young men to copywrite their material and look for ways to sell their writing, for litigation purposes.

Most of them were doing life sentences and did not realize their lyrics were given the same sentence if they could not free it from their own minds. Selling their material was one way of objectifying themselves into the Hip-Hop arena, making a name for themselves as a writer and another way of making money off lyrics.

I also got involved in Project Build's Legislative Action Committee. This committee concentrated on research, drafting, and presenting proposals to state legislators and community leaders for good time (time reduction for good behavior) for prisoners, based on an earned incentive allowance.

I got involved in other activities at Green Haven as well. I joined a long-term program in the Pre-Release Center, where we discussed ways of getting younger prisoners more involved in educational activities.

I was not just visible and articulate; I used my educational background and written skills to introduce and formulate ideas for change. I developed position papers, proposals, and action plans for a collective course of action based on organizational unity and streamlining our efforts. I argued for a coalition between older and younger prisoners. I constructed a Council of Elders concept, calling for older prisoners to become more active in teaching the younger ones.

Two facilitators of the Long Termer program developed a discussion forum and used it to bring prisoners to J-School for dialogue. I had accumulated most of the names for that forum and was an active participant.

But it didn't stop there. In time, I would find myself involved in developing a New Prison Movement.

Aside from my educational goals and service to others, I also devoted adequate time to prepare for my initial parole appearance. The violent nature of the crime I had been convicted of and my claim of innocence were the only strikes against me.

In the process of rallying community support, I received a letter from the prosecution's star trial witness, Maxine Bell (she had since gotten married and taken the last name Weber).

Her letter took me by surprise. I never expected to hear from the same person who had played a key role in my conviction. After her recantation, I assumed she had cleared her conscience and moved on with her life.

She wrote:

Hello Keith,

How are you?
 Well. I don't know where to start. I know that I am that last person that you want to hear from. Keith, I know that you hate a lot. I know you think that I am the worse person in the world right now.
 Keith, my Life is a living hell, but I am very sorry for what I did. But sorry is not good enough. Keith, I don't say much about what happen. I don't like to think about it. When I close my eyes at night, I see you!
 Keith, someone came up to me and said, 'do you remember about Keith Bush?' I died on the inside and dropped my head down. I said 'yes' with a tear in my eye. On Saturday, I was sitting in my living room, and you were on my mind, so I looked and there was a paper on my table, so I looked at it and I opened this paper, and I read it, and it was about you. I cried all day, [stayed] in the house all day, because I didn't know what to do.
 Keith, I'll be there when you go to court. I am not looking for you to write me back, but I am sorry for what happened. I am not asking you to forgive me, because if it was me, what would I do? I took your life from you. And I can't put back.

 I know that you are INNOCENT.

Maxine B. Weber

 After reading and rereading this letter, I felt some sympathy for Bell. I contemplated writing to her and encouraging her to move on with her life. Those old feelings of hatred for her because of her role in my conviction no longer existed.

I discussed the letter with my mother. Her first response was that we should help her. I knew my mother had suffered deeply due to her son being kidnapped by the justice system, and yet she still had forgiveness in her heart.

A member in one of the study groups suggested I should also reach out to Bell. Not to do so would contradict what we advocated. As a facilitator, I stressed the importance of reconciliation as an essential part of personal and collective transformation. Conflicts, disagreements, and tragedies are too burdensome to proceed in life without leaving room for atonement or forgiveness.

Besides, I had to come to terms with my own past feelings of hatred, hurt, pain and revenge. I knew those feelings had changed me.

Failure to at least consider forgiveness can lock us in a perpetual cycle of our own contradictions. I took on the personal responsibility to transform my thinking to improve my life, now I would be tested.

In making my decision, I encountered a lot of conflicting emotions. In the end, I reached out to the same person whose actions contributed to my deepest pain. It was the first clear indication to me of the benefits of my internal growth. There had been a time when I wouldn't have even considered it.

First, I sought professional advice and mediation as a healthy reconciliatory approach. But I didn't receive a favorable response. I decided to write directly to Bell. Through correspondence, I found a way to forgive her and encouraged her to put her life back together by moving on.

There was little left for me to accomplish after that to prepare for parole. I completed over fifty educational programs in about every subject the prison system offered. Some of them I facilitated. I was active in most organizational activities in my first twelve years at Green Haven.

I was a part of many group activities. I learned from and taught others. I engaged in the early Green Haven discussion panels. I aspired to leadership and had a positive effort at that facility and in my community.

My ideas, joined with those of my peers and community leaders, empowered many prisoners and others in the communities from which most of us came. I spent my time advancing my education, maintaining a good disciplinary record, and offering my service. I earned the respect of my peers, the facility administration, and leaders from the community.

At my initial parole appearance, I presented overwhelming family and community support, a place of residence, and employment opportunities. I submitted over two hundred petition signatures and thirty letters from family, professionals, and prominent community leaders.

Although the parole board considered me guilty, there was one thing they could not dispute: I was clearly not the same seventeen-year-old kid who had entered the prison system twenty years before.

Yet it was to no avail. By the parole interview, it was obvious the commissioners were only concerned with "the nature of the crime." They considered my achievements irrelevant. My parole denial was based on something they knew could not change.

The hurt and frustration I felt in the denial of my freedom is hard to explain. I had done everything I could and come so close to finally fulfilling the dream I had had for two decades. With a simple "no," my life was turned back into the nightmare I wanted so badly to wake up from.

It left me asking the same old question: Why me?

I was almost thrown back into my previous state of despair.

It would be just as difficult to overcome the reason for parole denial at my second parole appearance two years later.

The only required program I had refused to take part in was for sex offenders. I had no problem taking the program as a requirement for parole. But to enter this kind of program required a written admission of guilt. That was out of the question.

Without this program and an admission of guilt, the parole board would continue to deny me. I was in a catch-22. My dilemma raised serious concerns about whether I could look to parole as a viable option for release. I was ready to appear for a second time at the parole board. I still had my sanity and had achieved the things I needed to assist me in resocialization. But it was again irrelevant. My achievements and contributions were immaterial in the eyes of the commissioners. I was re-sentenced to serve an additional two years, the maximum allowed.

There is no way the parole board was going to consider my innocence. I was just hoping for them to be fair-minded in acknowledging my personal development as a requirement for release.

My parole was denied for a second time. It left me acutely distressed. If I could not overturn my conviction, I would die in prison. Under no circumstances would I stand before anyone and take the blame for this terrible crime. Not even in exchange for my release.

I had been denied parole on six occasions (twenty-four months between each). The reasons for denial were always for the nature of the crime and my refusal to admit guilt or submit to a program that required an admission of guilt.

The parole board had decided a claim of innocence was not acceptable.

Having appeared at six parole hearings made me familiar with parole expectations. By my third parole appearance, I understood what the parole board had in store for me. There was no need to prepare as hard for my third appearance as I had for the first two.

At this appearance, in November 1998, the parole board made it clear they had no intention of releasing me. The only possibility they left open to me was to admit to committing the crime and submit to being label a sex offender. The mere idea of this demand offended me deeply.

At this third parole appearance, I had been verbally attacked for maintaining my innocence. The fact that I had the nerve to take this stance enraged the presiding commissioner. He said the board had no interest in innocence and argued such foolishness would only bury me in the prison system.

This commissioner was only concerned with guilt and a detailed description of how and why the crime was committed. He expected me to provide him with insight into the psychological underpinnings of this kind of murder—as if I had any to give.

There was simply no way I could stand before anyone and play the role of the vicious killer. It made me feel as if all the time I spent in prison was nothing more than an extension of my precinct experience. I do not know which was worse: the trauma I encountered at the precinct or the possibility of dying in prison for a stance I should have held from the start. What I do know is there was something at my core dictating that stance. What the parole commissioners required of me was a parallel to what the homicide detectives had done to me physically and psychologically during the night of my arrest.

But I was not that boy. I was a full-grown man operating at a completely different level.

This was the most painful decision I ever had to make. I was willing to die in prison before taking somebody else's blame for the crime. I was willing to pay the price by aggressively opposing all who believed they had the right to define me.

The toughest part of dealing with parole denials was delivering the sad news to my loved ones. The disappointment was crushing. Hopefulness turned into helplessness. Anticipation turned into anguish. This was especially true in the case of my mother. Trying to explain away another setback left her sobbing, in fear that I might never leave prison alive… or that she might not live long enough to greet me.

The more my mother cried, the more I would rage inside. Her grief seized my entire being and perforated my soul.

Yet through it all, I was able to somehow convince her it would be all right. I tried to guide her to a temporary state of optimism so I too could renew my own strength and rationality. It was difficult explaining to my mother the harsh reality of my fate. How could I tell her that if this system had its way, I would probably die in prison?

I would also think about Sherese's mother, who never got the opportunity to see her daughter reach her sweet sixteen birthday.

It was rough living out my life away from the people I loved the most. Prolonged periods of imprisonment were erasing opportunities for the precious interactions that built family closeness and fond personal memories. My only memories were outdated mental images of loved ones who had grown older or passed away.

But even if I had been denied parole again, I knew I had to keep fighting. It was what motivated me. Holding onto my innocence was not the most difficult part of the struggle. Finding a way to prove it was. I just hoped the years I invested would bring my goal to fruition. I had no way of foreseeing the outcome, nor was I interested in trying to prove a point at the expense of wasting my life away inside a cage. Many people would warn me, "When is enough enough? Just admit to the crime and submit to whatever they want. You've already done the time. Life is too short and precious."

The truth is that who I had become couldn't countenance giving up. This experience molded me. Being what the criminal justice system wanted me to be was contrary to everything I was as a human being. How could I look any person in the eye with any degree of integrity if I let the criminal justice system take it away?

To be a real man, I must live, grow, and die according to my own beliefs about justice.

It was a tricky predicament to be in, but there are other situations far worse than mine. There's no reason to do a comparative analysis—we are all involved in our own struggles. Mine had its own purpose, which can best be summed with the words of former NAACP Julian Bond to the group's 92nd annual convention in 2001:

"It means at all times following your highest sense of right, whatever the consequences, however lonely the path, and however loud the jeers... It is holding on to the power of truth when everyone around you is accepting compromises."

My innocence has always been an essential part of my integrity. This integrity protects my sanity and defines my humanity. The mere idea of swallowing my dignity for a taste of freedom leaves a bitter taste in my mouth. Giving up my innocence would be like a righteous man giving up his passport into heaven. To voluntarily admit guilt to a senseless murder that I didn't commit would strip me of all my worth.

Why would any prisoner with a maximum sentence of life imprisonment knowingly give up this only option for parole?

There are only two sensible reasons: either that person is litigating, or that person is strongly opposed to admitting to a crime he or she did not commit.

How many prisoners in New York—or in the entire U.S.—have been punished for over a decade for continuing to maintain a claim of innocence? You can probably count them on one hand. But can you count one guilty prisoner who would subject themselves to this kind of unnecessary punishment if they were truly guilty? There is no benefit for the guilty to profess a claim of innocence.

Prior to trial in 1975, I had been given an opportunity to plead guilty to a lesser offense in exchange for a lesser sentence. If I were guilty, I would have accepted that plea and could have been home many years earlier.

Now, by maintaining my innocence, I was putting myself through the same amount of extra time I would have served if I had taken the plea—on top of the time I had already served.

In the end, the board's stance on innocence would extend my initial twenty-year minimum sentence to thirty-two years.

The DNA Dilemma

Centurion Ministries of Princeton, N.J. is a legal clinic that works on behalf of the innocent. In the latter part of the 1990s, Mary Ward, a worker at the clinic, convinced her staff to take on my case.

Members of the Ministries worked diligently on issues that could overturn my conviction.

Because of advancements in forensic science, we wanted to take a deeper look at medical records to see if there was a way to reexamine toxicological tests, fiber, or soil analyses, fingernail scrapings and more.

We filed a motion requesting copies of medical records. The medical examiner's office was willing to release medical records, but the district attorney's office was not. They wouldn't allow the medical office to even talk to us about the case. The motion was denied.

After working on this case for about five years, Centurion Ministries was unable to find any avenues for exoneration. There were just too many roadblocks at that time.

Around February 2001, the clinic came to a consensus that there was nothing else they could do to assist me. I remain forever thankful, particularly to Ward, for their effort and service.

In November the following year, the board of parole denied me parole for a fifth time, resentencing me to an additional two years. They again made it clear the only possibility for my release was for me to take full responsibility for the crime.

I firmly maintained my innocence, refusing to submit to their program requirements. My sentence of life imprisonment meant the board of parole could keep me in prison as long as it wanted if I continued to refuse to meet their terms for release.

During this period, I had no legal representation or money to hire an attorney. I lost all legal arguments at the state level and was denied entrance into the federal courts for review. All my efforts to reach out to legal clinics and organizations for assistance were to no avail.

I immediately went after the one thing a guilty person would never even consider touching: DNA.

DNA testing flourished after the 1991 Charles Dabbs case in New York in which a man convicted of rape was exonerated by DNA. It unlocked a new way of thinking across the board, even triggering advocacy for a moratorium on the death penalty.

DNA revolutionized public opinion, diluting the notion of near perfection earlier professed by America's justice system.

The increasing number of DNA exonerations served as a precedent for other states to follow. In response, some states went so far as to implement DNA review panels.

As head of the Suffolk County district attorney's office, the late James M. Catterson, Jr. was the first to establish a DNA review project in the Northeast. The intended purpose was to use DNA to reexamine old cases of persons who may have been mistakenly convicted.

I initially thought a review project by Suffolk County was a great idea. It showed an attempt to break from the long history of improper practices and foul play.

I knew if there was any DNA found in this case, the district attorney's office would gladly test it. Many of the staff were totally convinced I was guilty, though two were helpful. But what they didn't realize was I was more than willing to have my DNA tested. I knew DNA was a perfect way to prove my innocence.

Sherese had struggled with her killer(s). It was highly likely traces of the murderer's genetic profile would have lodged under her fingernails. All Sherese's clothes were preserved, as well as the scrapings from her fingernails.

There would have been sufficient biological material in the scrapings for a crime laboratory to obtain a DNA profile had testing been available at the time of the murder. It would still be possible today.

I contacted the district attorney's office in September 2001 for more information on the DNA program. In a letter of reply, assistant district attorney Kathleen McGovern wrote, "The only cases that can be reviewed are those in which DNA material was gathered at the crime scene and is presently in existence, and where all reasonable people agree that an exclusion would mean an exoneration of the convicted individual."

To me that meant if there was any DNA found and the district attorney was willing to test it, it would have to be considered strong enough to exonerate me. Obviously, that position would change when DNA found in this case excluded me.

I had my family make phone calls. I continued to write follow-up letters off and on for almost five years, practically begging the district attorney's office to search for DNA in this case.

In November 2005, they finally agreed to review my conviction under Suffolk county's DNA Review Project. I made a request that they test the metal afro-pick, the so-called weapon as well as all other physical evidence.

That same month, item 1 (victim's fingernails scrapings) was taken to the lab to be tested for the presence of biological material. My request for the metal pick was ignored.

Instead, item 13 (a black plastic pick/comb found at the crime scene) was supposed to be sent along with item 1 to the crime lab for DNA analysis. But the plastic pick wasn't sent until years later, when we submitted a motion for a second round of testing.

I was told I would be contacted by the district attorney's office when the results arrived.

What I didn't know—but was told when I made my request—was that the metal pick could not be tested. Why? Because in 1983 someone in the district attorney's office broke the seal on the box of physical evidence for this case. Whoever broke the seal took the metal pick out of the box and destroyed it. The box was then sealed again, leaving all the other physical evidence untouched.

To this day, I have not been given a reason as to why someone would destroy the supposed weapon.

On June 12, 2008, Yvonne I. Milewski, M.D., Chief Medical Examiner, informed us they were not in possession of any body fluids or tissue samples from Sherese.

Milewski said "toxicologic samples and formalin fixed tissues, which were previously stored, had also been destroyed." She did not say when this had happened.

The only tissues from the autopsy preserved by the Suffolk County medical examiner were fixed in formalin. These samples cannot produce genetic markers because they are stored in formaldehyde.

I know I am innocent! I requested all items be tested where the possibility of DNA might exist. I even asked them to test my DNA against any blood found on the deceased. I requested they reexamine her clothing for hair samples and test it against me.

The district attorney said the only evidence available for DNA testing were fingernail scrapings and a black plastic comb found at the crime scene. Those two items were supposed to have been sent to the lab for DNA analysis.

In April 2006, someone from the district attorney's office wrote to me that the lab would test "recovered biological material" found under Sherese's fingernails. I wrote back that same day, eagerly agreeing to submit a sample of my DNA for testing.

On May 6th, my DNA was swabbed and tested against this recovered biological material from the fingernail scrapings. The black plastic comb was not tested.

I sent another letter (this time notarized) consenting to give this sample and an acknowledgement that my DNA could be used for comparison in other unrelated open cases. The letter was accompanied by an enclosed consent form.

I ended my letter by stating, "I do acknowledge and emphatically encourage you to use my DNA for comparison in any unrelated open cases ever committed or committed in the future during my lifetime."

I was so happy they found something that could be tested. Their willingness to test it made me feel like I was finally on my way to exoneration.

A few months went by. I wrote numerous letters to the district attorney's office. Still no response. I wrote to Mr. Seligman, my trial attorney, asking for his assistance.

He immediately replied, promising to investigate the matter. This was a few months prior to my seventh parole appearance, scheduled for November 2006.

I finally received a letter from the district attorney's office regarding my request for the DNA results. It said I would be contacted when the results arrived.

To my surprise, I was also informed I would be appearing before the parole board in November of 2006—and would be released!

The board of parole is an independent body vested with its own decision-making power.

What did the district attorney's office know that I didn't?

The letter was confident. "You will be released." Not "might" or "should." Will.

On September 23rd, 2005, item #01.13 (microscopic slides containing victim's fingernail scraping) was resubmitted to the Suffolk County crime lab. This item yielded cellular material and was therefore prepared by forensic scientist Helen Lee-Wyss for DNA-STR analysis.

On September 8th, 2006, the results of the testing clearly established the DNA found underneath Sherese's fingernails did not match mine. In all the samples tested (#1.13.1, 1.13.2 and 1.13.3), I was excluded as a possible contributor.

It was conclusive: I could not have been the source of this DNA.

Item #1.13.1 contained a mixture from more than one person. It eliminated me as the source of that DNA mixture.

Item #1.13.2 contained DNA from more than two persons, including one male. But it also excluded me.

Item #1.13.3 contained a mixture of DNA from one female. That obviously wasn't me.

In addition to the single male DNA sample, there was material from two different females found under Sherese's fingernails. Who were these people?

One was presumably Sherese herself. The other could have implicated a female participant in her death. During my trial, there had been no evidence presented suggesting female participation. Even the prosecution had argued that I acted alone.

I never stopped reaching out for assistance. I didn't have the funds for legal representation, so I continued the fight on my own while petitioning post-conviction innocence clinics and other possible sources.

I was extraordinarily fortunate to receive a response from Professor Adele Bernhard at the Post-Conviction Innocence Clinic, who in 2007 was the legal director at Pace University in New York. She agreed to take my case.

We would soon be in for a long battle.

Bernhard is now a distinguished adjunct professor of law at the New York University School of Law. According to her, the students there are provided with hands-on experience by investigating criminal convictions like mine. They are required to track down court records, conduct interviews, and develop legal arguments.

In my ten-plus years with Bernhard's clinic, many of her students have come and gone. But all have made great efforts to uncover the truth of this case.

They spent many hours studying, researching, and assisting with the preparation of legal arguments in my favor. I am forever in debt to them all for their services.

I also obtained the support of a longtime friend who reappeared in my life. He was not at the party in 1975 and did not know much about the case. Minister Willie E. Chaplin and I grew up together in North Bellport. As teenagers, both of us often hung out together, playing basketball and interacting with other friends.

Our paths took different directions. Minister Chaplin eventually went on to pursue his education at the State University College at Buffalo in New York. A committed servant and devoted Christian, he lives on Long Island with his beautiful wife Regina.

Minister Chaplin and I reconnected, like divine intervention. It was at a unique time when everything was slowly coming together. All the different people who played a part have a reputation that rides on justice. Collectively, they opened the door for me in a strange way. God had sent me some angles.

I needed assistance from someone living on Long Island who knew the Bellport community and its people.

Chaplin would become a tremendous help to me and my attorney's staff by tracking down old names of people who attended the fateful party.

He devoted his own time, money, and effort making phone calls and traveling to speak personally with teenagers who have long since grown into adults.

The Worst Crime of All

Aside from genocide, slavery, and serial killing, there are no categories of crime as horrendous as sex offenses. The severity of these offenses is exacerbated when committed against minors.

Historically, some of the worst scars inflicted on the human psyche were left by sex offenders. The pages of history are swamped with despicable evidence of these crimes.

The massacre of men and vicious rape of women and young girls is an invention of no one country. Teens, both girls and boys, were used as sex slaves during slave-trades. Kidnappings and rapes were common practice by most conquerors.

One of Jesus's disciples, probably more than one prophet, and possibly several presidents of nations would have to register as sex offenders today.

Take a glimpse into America's past. Some of the very people commemorated and honored as patriotic heroes, leaders, even founding fathers have left DNA at crime scenes. Frown if you will. Honest historians will bear witness.

A book could be written on where these offenders can be found. The title of the book would be "Everywhere." On the first page: relatives, clergy, leaders, politicians, law enforcement, teachers, police, correction officers, athletes, entertainers, lay persons, school officials… the list would go on.

Peer deeper and you will find a time when all women shared oppression. In many cases, rape was only a crime when the accused was Black or poor.

Former New York Parole Commissioner Chris Ortloff made his living denying parole to inmates while hiding his own perverted crimes. This sex offender was eventually convicted and sentenced to ten years in federal prison. Had he chosen the right profession or enjoyed celebrity status, maybe he could have also circumvented prosecution with a covert settlement.

Can we say with any degree of certainty that these types of offenders can be rehabilitated?

The prison environment has its own culture. That culture defines for itself the codes of criminality. There are crimes that generate respect and others that are deemed unacceptable.

Most inmates pursue criminality out of socioeconomic necessity, survival, self-defense, revenge, recklessness, or that ridiculous thirst for recognition and/or reputation. Then there are the more serious offenses: premeditated murder, assault, kidnaping, torture. As gruesome as these harsher crimes are, some would argue they're more civilized than sex offenses. Even serial killers consider themselves one step above this group.

Some inmates would love to reduce the sex offender's recidivism rate if prison officials and society would be willing to look the other way.

Some sex offenders feel they are entitled to special rights of secrecy about their status, as if revealing their crimes to other inmates is more of a violation than what they did to their victims. Unfortunately, some of these same offenders try to minimize their own offenses, hoping to lessen the outrage over their own despicable actions.

It is true enough that some convictions should not be considered sex offenses. The consequences of the laws may be exaggerated when involving consensual sex between teens, for instance. In Oklahoma, a nineteen-year-old was sentenced to life for having consensual intercourse with his sixteen-year-old girlfriend. He was a victim of a law that punished him for their three-year age difference. When released, he would be classified as a sex offender.

Unfortunately, sometimes the innocent does become trapped under this sex offender label. There is no greater form of humiliation. Claims of innocence are ignored unless proven by DNA. Sometimes even that isn't enough. The Central Park Jogger case of the 1990s is a prime example. People like former Mayor Mike Bloomberg, former Police Commissioner Raymond Kelly, and former President of the United States Donald Trump remained in denial even after DNA exonerated all five of the accused men.

During my incarceration, almost all innocent prisoners were forced to complete their entire sentence for not admitting guilt or for refusing to participate in required "guilt admission" programs.

Worst of all were the handful serving life who faced the prospect of never being released. I was one of those prisoners.

I reappeared before the board of parole for a seventh time in November 2006. Once again, parole required an admission of guilt. They were not interested in my claim of innocence.

I explained I was currently awaiting the results of DNA testing I knew would exonerate me. One parole commissioner's response was, "That don't impress me."

So much for the district attorney's claim that I would be released. I left the hearing as disappointed as ever.

I don't know who I was more upset with—myself for wanting to believe what the prosecution told me or the parole board for its continued abstinence.

Three days later, I received my envelope with the decision. Most prisoners try to determine the decision by the weight of the envelope. If an appeal is inside, the envelope will weigh more.

The light weight of the envelope sent shockwaves through my body.

I immediately opened the envelope.

I was granted parole!

Soon I would learn that granting me parole was not the same as granting me my freedom. The chairman/parole commissioner Robert Dennison amended my parole decision to impose additional restrictions upon me. Parole granted the New York State Board of Examiners the power to brand me as a sex offender.

The Board of Examiners deliberately undermined New York State Penal Law Section 70.30(1)(A) to classify me under this status. That law was created to determine eligibility for parole.

The attempted sexual abuse conviction only carried four years and was over in 1980. They used the murder conviction to tower over the lesser offense and then applied Section 70.30 retroactively to me.

Because of the seriousness of these types of offenses, the Board of Examiners knew they could violate the ex post facto clause, my equal protection rights, and the Fourteenth Amendment of the United States Constitution.

The Board of Examiners relied solely upon the attempted sexual abuse conviction to brand me. They placed me in the same category with the worst type of sex offenders. They branded me with this nasty label so that they could own me for the rest of my life.

Obviously, the moral responsibility to create and enforce laws that protect the most vulnerable is a social obligation. My objection is not to the creation of laws that prioritize the safety of women and children. Abuse of the innocent also requires protection.

Parole was fully aware of my stance. They were making me pay the heaviest price for maintaining this claim. Parole knew I was in the federal court seeking constitutional protection for my claim of innocence and petitioning the district attorney office begging them to test my DNA against any physical evidence found in this case. I do not fit in the same category of those who stood before parole and admitted to guilt.

I refused a guilty plea offer for a lesser-degree offense for a shorter incarceration just prior to trial. I would have been released from prison years before Megan's Law was passed, which had sex offender information available to the public. I would also have completed any maximum sentence on parole because the plea bargain did not carry a lifetime parole supervision.

Innocent prisoners, if unsuccessful in overturning their convictions, are also subject to the same requirements for release as the guilty. Therefore, almost all inmates (innocent or guilty) will stand before parole and take full responsibility for whatever they have been convicted of.

For the innocent person with a life sentence, admitting to a crime they did not commit after doing the time is their only hope for release. It's an abuse to force innocent prisoners to stand before the parole board and require them to pretend to be guilty in the hope of earning release.

My case was extreme. Each time the board mandated an admission, I maintained my innocence. The board could have, if it chose, indefinitely denied me parole for the rest of my life. They made this undeniably clear to me. Parole was also made aware that my stance will remain the same.

If I had stood before them and pretended to have committed the crime, they would have been within their rights to brand me with such nasty labels and subject me to stringent conditions.

Yet twelve years after my minimum sentence was over, the parole board suddenly reversed course, bypassing their requirement for admission of guilt. In November 2006, parole made an exception for me. They released me under my claim of innocence.

I stood before the Board of Parole for a seventh time, and again denied being a murderer and sex offender.

Whatever the reasons, their decision to release me was not a clear acknowledgement of acceptance of innocence. The requirements for my release were in the same category as those for the guilty. Why was an exception made to release me when I never pretended to be the horrible person the criminal justice apparatus had dubbed me?

One thing was certain: granting me parole was not based on the idea that "enough is enough." I know a few prisoners in New York (both those who admit guilt and those who maintain innocence) still being denied parole after having spent twenty-plus years beyond the minimum.

It probably didn't start with me. But shortly after I was released, I was glad to read that the New York State Division of Parole was finally granting parole to at least some prisoners who continued to maintain their innocence.

Some of these innocent prisoners with lifetime parole supervision were having their parole ended after three years. I wasn't one of them. I stayed on parole for over a decade.

My parole was granted in the same year the DNA results came in. It was also the same year I was pursuing a federal lawsuit that put the parole requirement of guilt on a collision course with my First Amendment right to religious freedom.

The lawyers representing me in both these separate cases, for their own reasons, believed one or the other had a lot to do with me making parole.

The justice system used the sex offender registry to deceive people into believing I was one of the worst individuals in this world. But you will not read in their registry that parole went against their own requirements to release me by not mandating that I admit to being a sex offender.

What you will read is how they removed the "attempt" from their registry of "sexual abuse" to imply there is "evidence" that a sexual crime was committed in this case.

There was no rape kit performed in this case or any physical evidence of the deceased being sexually assaulted. There was no physical evidence to support any type of sexual assault by anyone.

Parole and the Board of Examiners used public fears and hatred to define me. These agencies succeeded in creating a negative public perception about me that did not tell the true story.

They maliciously blocked me from using my abilities to create a normal life for myself. My potential was still confined, my humanity enslaved. It was another attempt to ensure I would never experience happiness or have the status of an ordinary citizen. They put this in place for the rest of my life, making sure I would never know what it really feels like to be free.

Every three years, a parolee on lifetime parole supervision can have his or her parole terminated. Most parolees are automatically freed from parole after their first three years on parole.

This includes parolees with extensive criminal records and some with multiple murder convictions. I was one of the handful of parolees denied all my three-year reviews for no justifiable reason.

There was literally nothing in my behavior or lifestyle that supported the conditions they continued to place on me.

In my sixty-one years on this planet, outside of this crime that I did not commit, I have never been involved in, accused of, or charged with any kind of criminal act whatsoever.

And they would know if I had been. My DNA remains in the state and federal databases so it can be matched to any unsolved crimes.

Some of the restrictions I was forced to live under were worse than being in prison. In some ways, though, I was fortunate for having been paroled to my place of birth in Bridgeport, Connecticut.

Most of my parole officers were open-minded and fair. They all gave me an opportunity to make a successful transition.

They had been made aware of my firm stance of innocence and willingness to litigate on those grounds. Some even encouraged me to continue to fight for my exoneration.

I knew I could not afford to drown in the negative stigma inflicted upon me. I just kept fighting. Writing a book and telling my side of the story is part of that.

Even writing has cost me. My only parole violation in the ten years since being released was for using a computer to write this book without first seeking permission.

I was locked back up for the violation, imprisoned for over a year.

I was granted parole back to the same state and parole officer. He apologized to me, because he said he didn't realize until after the fact that he had overreacted.

But I had no regrets. I took full responsibility for my actions.

He gave me permission to use a computer, to go on the internet and have email accounts. I am glad he did; there was nothing that was going to stop me from telling my side of this story and fighting to prove my innocence. Not even a parole violation.

God, the Holy Bible, and The Trial Oath

New York state's Board of Parole was not the only agency retaliating against me for maintaining my innocence. The New York Department of Correctional Services (now called New York State Department of Correctional Services and Community Supervision, or NYSDOCCS) herein referred to as "Corrections," also engaged in this assault.

In 2000, a Corrections counselor at Fishkill Correctional Facility began warning me of the consequences for refusing to meet new mandatory program requirements. This policy was implemented specifically to impose an admission of mandate on any person in New York state convicted of a sex offense.

I have always made it clear that I had no problem taking a program required by parole, but if that program required an admission of guilt for completion, I would not even consider it regardless of the consequences. I only rejected the onslaught imposed upon me for maintaining my innocence.

It was just a matter of time before I would be the next one to transfer. This transfer became their way of further punishing me for being innocent. Lowering my classification status was the tool used.

At this level, there was a policy by Corrections, backed by legislation, that was enforced upon the innocent. That policy was waiting for me. But for me, this transfer became just another battleground.

Upon my transfer to Fishkill prison, I was told about a policy mandating that I submit to guilt or face the consequences of being moved hundreds of miles away from my family until I did so.

The Fishkill counselors I was assigned to called me to his office to inform me of the program called "Denial" prisoners who claimed to be innocent and those still appealing their cases were taking to at least knock out the Closer to Home Policy, approved by central office.

The program only allowed for program satisfaction but would not be considered by parole as a requirement for release. Rendering the transfer punishment policy for mandatory programming no longer applicable. I heard of the denial program. There were prisoners who were innocent who took the program. If there were no requirements for admission, I thought it was a good idea.

I was placed on a transfer to Gowanda Correctional Facility in far western New York. At that facility, I was informed by the counselor that he had signed me up for a sex offender program. There was no such thing as a denial program, and admission of guilt was a requirement. One prisoner told me Gowanda was a sex offender facility. The officers were rotten toward prisoners who signed out or got kicked out of the program. They also sent prisoners to the super-max special housing unit (the Box) who refuses. I just looked at him and told him, "Good, because I'm signing myself out of this place first thing in the morning."

The next day, I signed myself out of the program. I was placed under keep-lock for refusal.

I was sentenced to sixty days in Corrections super-max special housing unit for refusing. After completing my sixty days in confinement, I was transferred to Wyoming Correctional Facility, near Attica in New York. In Wyoming, I was informed I could no longer transfer to any prison close to my family because Corrections punished prisoners who refused participation in mandatory program.

This policy was a mandate created for medium status inmates but did not apply to prisoners in maximum security facilities. They moved me to a minimum facility to impose this restriction upon me and buried me upstate.

When the facility imposed this new policy upon me, only one thing came to mind: parole had no intent to release me, and now Corrections was trying to destroy my family ties by keeping me in a facility over 376 miles away from my family as a form of punishment for maintaining my innocence.

But what they didn't know was that by placing me in a predicament that made it difficult to be able to see my loved ones, or effectively litigate this case, I was ready to fight.

Like David, I learned—there was only one way to defeat Goliath: with the help of God.

The need for spiritual enhancement often comes to us during difficult times. In my situation, I needed to take the initiative, and if a blessing were to come (as it did), I hoped that blessing was a testament to the choices I made during that difficult journey.

There would come a time when I realized the need to embrace my spirituality and to search for the essence of what and how that spiritual integrity should be applied to me.

I used my imagination like a canvas with a psychic screen. On that screen, I painted my own reality contrary to the picture painted by the educational and other systems that shaped me. My soul became my spiritual vehicle used for mental travel and physical projection. My expedition was to find my rightful place in the seat of power. The willpower.

Coming to terms with an infinite source of God-Consciousness reconnected me to my core. It also sparked a flame of awareness that fueled me and nurtured my faith in divine guidance and deliverance.

It enabled me to perceive a divine presence outside of human favoritism. I needed to perceive God as an infinite source of capacity from which to draw, not blame, for a reality created by the choices made by human decisions and actions, not divine dictation.

The allegories in religious texts passed down, interpreted, and delivered to us by past and present teachers did not provide the fulfillment I needed to make sense of my own definition of who and what God is to me. I was not interested in being spoon-fed ideas about a God consciousness I believe would always exist beyond human comprehension. I reserved the right to question, even within my own faith, anything contrary to and the difference between what was rational, factual, or faithful.

As a neophyte with intense curiosity, I loved engaging in the exercise of foolishly hoping I could somehow peek into that inner realm of reality to bear witness to the presence of the omnipotent. As foolish as it sounds, stretching my imagination in search of the unknown broadened my perspective and objectified my views.

Locked up in cages for decades allowed for plenty of idle time and quiet moments to search and reflect. My approach to self-development was initially internal. It is where I would find my greatest peace and a self-love that rendered the hatred for me by so many people in this world irrelevant.

In the mental world, all power flows through imagination. I used my imagination to create a psychological place where I could draw power from a link connected to what I would perceive as a God infinite source of capacity. I used my imagination as a portal to travel to a self-created empty place of calmness for meditation before prayer. I called this place "Medi-Prayer."

It would become a special place where I could rid myself of my mental armament and bathe again in the serenity of inner grace.

This is where I made my request for guidance and for regeneration in preparation for my return to this physical life in which a criminal injustice system had enslaved me.

Meditation cleanses, relaxes, and equips my mind for travel. Before I start my mental travel in preparation for entrance into the dream state, I use the force in breath to cleanse and heal my entire body, to leave it in good health and recognition for my return.

To enter my state of Medi-Prayer at bedtime, I would lay comfortably relaxed with eyes closed. I'd take a moment to physically relax the body and begin my breathing exercise. I would imagine each inhaled breath, carrying with it a magnetizing and healing power. Inhaling was my way of taking in imaginary healing power and releasing that power to the entire body for the purpose of consuming all negative forces/energies within the body to be released in exhale. Imaginary healing power was my way of soothing the body with vitality and strength upon my departure into the dream state.

After the exercise and the mental achievement of relaxation with eyes closed, I would imagine myself mentally traveling to the region of the pituitary gland. There is where I would turn all attention inward until I reach the state of total mental darkness.

Pitch darkness becomes my screen and the place for Medi-Prayer. It's a purely imaginary state where relaxation is embraced, prayer for divine guidance in exchange for my daily good deeds and blessings are offered. This is where I would await my spirit to take me into the dream state where the answers reside.

This was the kind of thinking that would ultimately heal my spirit, mind, and body and helped me to discover and develop the roadmap that has led to victory.

When we discover and embrace that inner voice within, I believe answers will follow.

But if I continued to look for answers through anger, rage, and negativity, the answers would remain unseen. Medi-prayer became the region and I the visitor where I could open my mind and connect with those inner portions of the self.

Before I enter the mental realm, I always quote from Proverbs 29:18: "Where there is no vision, the people perish." To me, vision is everything. Without it, we can't even perceive that which we believe as faith. Vision is sight, comprehension is its light.

My vision showed me answers in the form of intuition, insight, rationality, and logic, even in tragedies or in my own failures and suffering. Some were sent to me in daydreams and nighttime dreams. Some came as examples from nature.

Most came in times of contemplation and quietness.

When you are up against a powerful force like the criminal justice system, you need to not only believe in yourself but to believe in a God-power stronger than any force of injustice created by man.

I did my best work in my quiet moments. There were many nights when I quietly lay in a cage, relying on that inner voice to bring me answers. The answers were always there. It was my responsibility to find and materialize them. To do so, I had to search to find the answers wherever they were.

As I prayed and deliberated on a course of action, I kept having this strange feeling I was right for what I was doing: hold my stance and the answers would follow. I needed to be open-minded in my search. I believe the Creator loves to test our faith by answering our requests but leaving it up to us to pursue them.

I found my answer from my educational experience in the Malcolm X Black Studies program. But the main part of the answer, I retrieved from reading the Bible and Medi-prayer.

Many times, I stood in courtrooms while my fate was being decided by others. I had no idea the courtroom was placed upon the very foundation of religious judgment in the fate of heaven or hell. Bring God and the Bible into the court room was deliberately designed to hold an accuser accountable to God as well. This connection to the American courtroom structure cannot be denied. Could this be why the trial oath is administered before the holy Bible and in God's name? Isn't there supposed to be a separation of church and state?

In the United States, a person's fate, in the physical world is not only a way of administering judgment upon those accused of committing sin against man's laws, socially, but it is a fate that awaits us in judgment against God's commandments, religiously. If God's named is used in vain.

The Ten Commandments from the Biblical text in the Old Testament in the Book of Exodus clearly states: "Thou shalt not take the name of the Lord thy God in vain; for the LORD will not hold him guiltless that taketh his name in vain" (Exodus 20:7).

Why are we instructed to raise our right hand before the Bible and swear to tell the truth in God's name?

The Bible contains the Lord's commandments. One specifically warns us not to use the name of the Lord in vain. If we testify "in God's name," we must testify to the truth, because the Lord will not hold us guiltless if we misuse God's name.

The American court system commits us to that commandment and therefore holds us accountable to God in the hereafter.

By raising my right hand, I was, in a way, using my religious faith as a conveyor to God that made me accountable to what I testified to under oath. That is a serious pledge of accountability. Is this why the Third Commandment is embodied in the trial oath? The courts know you may be able to fool them or a jury, but you cannot fool God.

In 1976, the court system made me accountable to God by transforming my trial testimonial oath into a holy pledge. Two decades later, the court would have to decide if they would now protect my right to uphold what I testified to in God's name under the banner of my religious faith.

I brought this issue before the federal courts, demanding protection of my right to religion and to stop Corrections from retaliating against me for exercising that right.

It was time for the court to decide. I immediately went after corrections with the intent of using a court victory against the Parole Board. Parole had more power than Corrections, and the parole commissioners I stood before made it clear to me. They expressed no concerns about my innocence or commitment to God or the Bible. As far as they were concerned, I was convicted of this crime and therefore was guilty of the crime.

Initially, I wrote directly to Corrections Commissioner Glenn S. Goord with my concerns. I requested he make an exception that would allow me to exercise my constitutional right to uphold my religious faith, based on my testimony of innocence, free from retaliation.

I didn't request to be transferred to a medium-security facility, so I asked that I be allowed to transfer back to a maximum-security prison where the "closer to home" policy didn't apply.

I also made it clear that my Parole requirements for release condemned me to die in a cage and this policy is nothing but a terroristic form of coercion that can be and will be used against me if I am able to overturn my conviction. The commissioner didn't even consider my request.

I wasn't interested in making a legal issue out of it. I did not want to open a door for guilty prisoners to escape from their rehabilitative responsibilities. I was hoping the commissioner would allow me to transfer back closer to home. This would put me in a better position to maintain family ties and to investigate/litigate this case.

I had already made my position clear to Parole and Corrections. I just wasn't going to take any programs that required an admission of guilt. The commissioner ignored my plea for a rational resolution.

In February 2003, I filed a grievance, an administrative remedy that is required before court litigation, challenging Corrections for punishing me for upholding my faith in God by exercising my right to religion. After a grievance, one of the grievance representatives approached me in the yard.

Impressed with my argument, he secretly provided me with more information and names of prisoners (all White in residence of predominately White upstate rural communities) who were released from Wyoming without having to take this program. In these cases, there were no claims of innocence. I used it to file a second grievance.

In my research in preparation for this lawsuit, I had also discovered the same lies by counselors about other prisoners similarly situated. In a few of these affidavits submitted in the lawsuit, I discovered there was in fact a sex offender denial program.

That program was for inmates still appealing their conviction according to the affidavit. After the completion of the denial program, the sex offender program was still mandatory.

In another affidavit, an innocent inmate was placed under so much pressure by the Corrections and Parole program mandate, he suffered a heart attack and almost died because of medical mistakes.

I also produced affidavits from prisoners threatened with violence by Wyoming prison for petitioning this issue.

I would also learn that the policies for the sex offender program were never adhered to. There was federally funded training mandated for counselor instructors. "There appears to be a coverup about the credentials of counselors. The program was federally funded and neither accredited nor fraud used to defraud the regulations," according to another affidavit.

From the grievance representative, I also learned that the defendants named in the lawsuit were violating their own policies. Grievances weren't sent to the facility superintendent as required by law. They were systematically denied by the supervisor of the Inmate Grievance Program Committee.

I was able to get one of the inmate representatives to exchange the ribbon from the very typewriter in the Grievance Supervisor's office used to type up all denials (including mine), pretending it was coming directly from the superintendent's office.

After I got the ribbon and sent it out of the facility, I filed a grievance against the supervisor and would eventually name him in the lawsuit. I knew he wouldn't admit violating the grievance mechanism.

I had the proof (of which he was unaware), and now I had him on record deliberately lying. I was going to let him lie under oath before I exposed him in a court of law.

In 2003, I brought a civil action (42 USC section 1983) against the Commissioner of Corrections, the Superintendent of Wyoming Prison, Wyoming's Deputy Superintendent for Programs, Senior Correction Counselor, and Supervisor of the Inmate Grievance Program.

Two months after the filing of this complaint, I amended it to include another prisoner as a strategic indicator for class action invitation.

If you read the case in *Bush vs. Goord*, 1:03-CV-759S, you will be shocked to learn how Corrections secretly violated its own policies and laws with no regard for public safety.

In litigating this case I was able to show how Corrections was granted federal dollars for specific training of counselors to administer the program to improve public safety. These counselors were never trained and only began their training when it was first exposed in the Bush vs. Goord case. The more I investigated, the more violations I found.

I was able to obtain a lot of information about the sex offender program at Wyoming facility because that was the prison where most of the prisoners were sent as a punishment for refusing to surrender their claim of innocence. When they became aware of my complaint, some of them came forward with information they hoped I could use to fight this issue.

It was also the prison where these men were being threatened, intimidated, and their convictions exposed when challenging these issues. I know that to be a fact because they tried to do that to me. Until they realized how determined I was. I was coming after everybody who was trying to undermine me, including a security sergeant and his gang members who thought they could intimidate me like the others.

In 2005, the attorney general moved to dismiss the case under summary judgment. Summary judgment is a judgment by a court for one party against another party without a full trial.

We survived the summary judgment motion, and then the attorney general began litigating the case differently. At one point, his office was even willing to look at a possible settlement behind closed doors.

But in November 2006, I was granted parole. The federal district court made me moot (no longer relevant) in the complaint and dismissed my name from the case as one of the petitioners.

Anthony Bennett, the other petitioner in the case, was offered a settlement but chose not to compromise. He proceeded for monetary damages, according to the attorney who represented us. I had no further contact with Bennett to confirm or dispute that.

The case against Bennett was dismissed. He didn't demonstrate any apparent religious sincerity. I always thought only God could determine what's in or not in one's heart.

If it had been me in his place, I would have hollered so loud it would have caused an earthquake in the religious communities.

An institution like the criminal justice system should not be allowed to hide behind God when all it does is practice hypocrisy.

It is ironic how witnesses in this case had knowingly given false testimony with no concern for their own testimonial oaths in God's name.

Maxine Bell was the only witness, in this case, to stand in the same court of law to make amends for her misdeeds, even when faced with the threat of perjury and all that she lost.

She freed herself from the violation of using God's name in vain and has reestablished God's trust. The others who lied and will not make amends—their fates await them in judgment.

Who Killed Sherese Watson: The Search for Closure

This satellate map raises serious questions about the John Jones story. What about the other investigative leads that also raises serious questions?

Figure 2: Locations on 1978 Street Grid – Satellite Map

In the 1990s, over ten years after his release, Frank Turner contacted a family member of mine and gave them a number for me to contact him. According to the message, he had some important information about the case.

I assumed it had something to do with the boys from the red car. When I finally made the call, it turned out to be something entirely different.

The first thing Turner said was, "Keith, I know who killed Sherese."

Before I could reply, he continued, "It wasn't Rawleigh and them," referring to the boys in the red car.

Then he gave me a name. Keith Taylor.

I immediately responded, "Keith Taylor, who the fuck is that?"

"He's my wife's brother. He lived right around the corner from Sherese."

Turner told me the whole story.

As I listened in silence, I assumed this was just another rumor. There were so many contradictory rumors that it was hard to tell which had any substance.

When Turner got out of prison, he wanted to travel south to visit his daughter, who lived with Taylor's sister and other family members. Taylor ran into Turner around that time. They decided to make the trip together.

According to Turner, Taylor was extremely stressed out during the trip. They got into a deep conversation, which eventually led to Taylor breaking down and confessing that he was the one who killed Sherese.

Taylor was deeply in love with Sherese and wanted her for himself. Apparently, the feelings weren't mutual. The way Turner told me the story, it sounded like one of those "if I can't have you, then no one can" situations.

Turner was a role model for Taylor. He must have felt a need to confide in him. For years, he had been having difficulties dealing with what he allegedly had done.

At one moment, according to what Turner told me, Taylor briefly even contemplated turning himself in. But he obviously had a change of heart.

After Turner described all this, I had no idea what to think. I felt strange.

But what about the boys in the red car? Everything seemed to point to them. I owed it to Sherese to at least see if there was any substance to these claims.

I didn't want to expose the information and risk running Taylor away. We hired the law firm of C. Vernon Mason, Esq., who was at the time deeply engulfed in the Tawana Brawley case. Brawley, who was Black, had alleged that she'd been sexually assaulted at the age of fifteen by four White men. The case had gained national attention. The law firm was heavily involved in that case, so we pursued the private investigation route. We located the whereabouts of Keith Taylor.

I did my own digging and found out something from Stephinie, the female who introduced Sherese to me. Taylor, Sherese, and Stephinie smoked marijuana in Sherese's basement together. According to Stephinie, Taylor lived around the corner from Sherese and was in love with Sherese. She was not in love with him.

But I was still unable to determine if Taylor attended the party on the night of the murder. The people I asked couldn't remember.

Back on March 20th, 1997, at eleven a.m., I had watched about ten minutes of the *Jerry Springer Show* before being locked in my cell for the prison count. The television attracted a crowd of prisoners; there was an apparent fight about to escalate between Black Israelites and members of the Ku Klux Klan on the discussion panel.

What I didn't know was that one of the Black Israelites on the panel was Keith Taylor. Turner later sent word to me that he had seen Taylor on the show.

By that time, though, Turner had fallen victim to street life. The private investigator who believed he may have located Taylor was unsure how to approach him because of the alleged radical stance of Black Israelites toward White people.

A decade after my conviction, Georgette Farmer, a defense witness, resurfaced. Under the freedom of information law, in 1989, I made a request to the Suffolk County district attorney's office for my complete file. Years later, I would discover my complete file had not been sent to me.

There were two reports that referred to Georgette. One came from witness Don Copeland, who stated he saw Sherese when she came into the party with Brenda Carlos. He was later outside and saw Sherese come out with Georgette. Another report was from Georgette's mother, Doris Farmer. She had said Georgette and another girl, Malvina Griffin, had received telephone call threats that consisted of a male voice saying, "You'll be next."

Doris Farmer approached her daughter about reporting the telephone calls to the police, but her daughter declined.

These threats were serious. For years, my curiosity disturbed me with questions like:

What did Georgette and Malvina know that made someone want to quiet them by using the threat of murder?

Who was making these threats?

Why did the prosecution withhold this information from the defense?

Why didn't Georgette reveal the threats to the defense when we questioned and used her as a witness at trial?

What was she hiding, or who was she afraid of?

The need to answer these questions would fade over time. At that time, I was unable to find anything to take me further.

My release from prison did not in any way alter my determination to exonerate myself. If anything, I fought harder from the outside than I had while in prison.

I collaborated with my lawyer and the students from the Elisabeth Haub School of Law at Pace University, investigating rumors, looking for new evidence, following leads, and tracking down people we hadn't previously known attended the party.

Two of these people, Darlene Rush (the younger sister of defense witness Nora Rush) and Andrea Arnold (now Minister Andrea Smith), provided us with some interesting leads.

Both claimed they were with Sherese at Darlene's house earlier that evening before the party started. While Andrea waited for Darlene to get dressed, Sherese left alone after all three girls had agreed to meet up at the party to celebrate two of their birthdays.

Andrea's birthday was on the night of the party (January 10th), and Darlene's birthday was the next day (January 11th).

Later that night, the other two girls did meet up with Sherese at the party. They danced. They interacted with Sherese and other friends. When Sherese went outside, Darlene and Andrea followed her.

Outside, Darlene asked Sherese where she was going. Sherese told them she was going to have some fun and asked the two girls if they wanted to come. They followed her to a red car. Sherese climbed into the back seat. The two women told us that upon approaching the car, they looked inside. They saw Georgette Farmer in the front seat, a male driver, and two male individuals in the back.

Andrea said she spoke briefly with Georgette before Andrea and Darlene declined the invitation to go with them. The car drove off as the two girls reentered the party.

Darlene and Andrea claimed they gave a statement to detectives after Sherese's body was discovered. Both were told they would have to testify at the trial and would be notified.

They were never notified. The statements they gave to detectives are no longer a part of the prosecution's files since they had not sent to me my 1989 Freedom of Information request.

I spoke with Darlene on the phone. She was the one who told me about Georgette's dislike for Sherese. In one phone conversation, Darlene told me, "One day, I brought Sherese with me to Georgette's house to hang out. When Georgette saw Sherese with me she pulled me to the side and asked me why I brought her. Once Georgette found out Sherese was with me, she made up an excuse not to hang out with us. So, me and Sherese left."

Darlene said she never understood why Sherese went with her. She said she did not know if Sherese knew of Georgette's dislike toward her. Darlene also said she didn't believe Georgette was involved in the murder. She did think Georgette knew more but didn't understand why she wouldn't free herself from the burden of suppressing the truth.

Darlene was surprised when I told her Georgette said Sherese was her best friend. That Georgette was so traumatized by Sherese's murder she sought counseling for years. That she named one of own daughters after Sherese.

Andrea told me about a conversation she'd had with Malvina Griffin weeks after the murder. Before breaking down in tears, Malvina told Andrea she had to leave town and not to tell anyone she was going to New York City to hide out.

Malvina claimed something terrible had happened. Andrea was trying to find out what it was. But Malvina told her she didn't want to get Andrea involved.

Malvina also told Andrea "They were watching her" and that a boy called her house and said, "They'll kill me and anyone with me." Malvina was afraid for her safety.

Andrea believes Malvina's stepmother, Alice Griffin (now remarried), may be the only person who could tell us more about what Malvina was hiding.

This was interesting. Andrea could not have known about a police report with reference to Georgette and Malvina receiving threats. Andrea had never seen Malvina in the car with Georgette on the night of the party, so she couldn't have made the connection on her own.

When I told Andrea that Georgette had testified during the trial that she hadn't seen Sherese at the party, Andrea was incredulous. She asked for my permission to try to locate

Georgette. Andrea finally obtained Georgette's phone number and immediately contacted her. According to Andrea, the conversation went as follows:

After small talk, Andrea talked about the night of the party and questioned Georgette about seeing her inside a red car with three teenage boys as Sherese got in. Georgette said she couldn't remember much about the night of the party but denied being in the red car. She told Andrea she was with her boyfriend, Larry McMillian, in a red and white car.

Georgette emphasized being traumatized by what happened to Sherese and said she had to receive counseling. She said Sherese was her best friend. This was the reason she named one of her daughters after Sherese.

After further conversation, Georgette did admit that she and her boyfriend dropped Sherese off somewhere but couldn't remember the place. She also couldn't remember if there were other boys in the back seat. Later in the conversation, she said she thinks the boys were her boyfriend's cousins.

Georgette did say she didn't know why they arrested me because I didn't have anything to do with Sherese's death. Georgette told Andrea she was willing to help in any way and agreed to talk with my attorney.

My attorney contacted Georgette. In that conversation, Georgette said she didn't really remember if Sherese left the party with her and McMillian. She told my lawyer she felt as if Andrea was pressuring her, so she went along with it.

I wasn't sure what to make of all this. It was inconsistent with Georgette's and Chris Foster's original statements to detectives. Those statements had also been inconsistent with portions of their own trial testimony. Georgette had testified at trial that she'd arrived at the party about ten p.m. with her boyfriend Larry McMillian and Chris Foster in a red and white Malibu Classic.

Georgette got out of the car and talked with some people for about ten minutes, then got back into the car. She didn't see Maxine Bell at all that night or talk to Maxine sitting on the hood of her boyfriend's car, contrary to Bell's testimony, later recanted.

Donny Maynes came up to their car, got into an altercation with Foster, and threw a punch. McMillian slammed the door and pulled off. He took Georgette home. They had been at the party no longer than half an hour.

In cross-examination, Georgette told the prosecution she never saw Sherese or me at the party and could not remember if Malvina Griffin drove with them to the party. Georgette did claim she may have seen Malvina earlier during the day.

Georgette was questioned about a written statement she gave to detectives at her home on January 22nd. McMillian was also present at that time. In that statement, she claimed Sherese came by her house to see if she was going to the party. Georgette replied she didn't think she was.

According to Georgette's statement, she went to the party at nine p.m. with her sister Jeanette, Griffin, Foster, and McMillian. Jeanette and Malvina went into the party upon arrival. Georgette stayed outside, where she saw Sherese talking to some people.

In that statement Georgette said she only stayed at the party for twenty minutes before leaving for her house with McMillian and Foster. She didn't return to the party.

Chris Foster had testified he went to the party with Georgette, Griffin, and McMillian at about nine p.m. Georgette had tried to go inside, but someone wouldn't let her in. She came back to the car and asked Foster to walk her back to the door. Foster walked her to the door and waited for Georgette to come back. Then they both returned to the car. A few guys came over and forced their way into McMillian's car. They wanted to fight Foster. There was an argument. McMillian slammed the door, spun around, and left.

Foster did not see me, Sherese, or Bell at all that night. He did recall seeing Sherese earlier, at around eight p.m. She was by herself and walking toward the party.

Foster spoke with her for about five or ten minutes at the intersection of Mead and Brookhaven avenues. This was the same area where her body was found two days later.

In cross-examination, Foster was questioned about a statement he gave to police on January 14th. According to that statement, Foster had been at Jeanette's house with McMillian, Georgette, and Griffin.

Jeanette wanted to go to the party, so all five of them got into McMillian's car and went. It was around nine-fifteen p.m. They did not stay. They dropped Jeanette off and left. McMillian drove Foster to the house of another girl, Shirley Brennan. At about ten-fifteen p.m., Foster and Brennan walked back to Jeanette's house. On the way, they saw Sherese. They stopped to talk with her. Sherese told them she was on her way to the party.

Foster stayed at Jeanette's house for a little while before leaving for a friend's house in Patchogue, New York. He stayed there for the rest of the night.

McMillian was interviewed by detectives after Sherese's body was found. He claimed he did not attend the party but stayed across the street talking to a friend, Roosevelt Sims, who lived in the house opposite the party.

At about eleven p.m., Donny Maynes started "fooling around" with his car, and a minor argument ensued. McMillian decided he better bring Georgette home. He later went back to Sims's house.

McMillian said he had seen the red Barracuda parked in front of the party at about eleven p.m. He also saw it driving down the street several times during the night.

There was something about McMillian that didn't sit right. He wouldn't testify for the defense when he knew Maxine Bell was prepared to give false testimony against me. For some reason, he was also against me.

Was McMillian, a twenty-one-year-old guy manipulating these two fifteen-year-old girls (Georgette and Maxine) behind the scenes?

McMillian would eventually leave Georgette for Maxine. He went out of his way to take good care of Maxine. He married her, and they moved to Alabama. When Maxine first told her husband about her intentions of going back to New York to tell the truth about her false testimony against me, McMillian had a fit. He was so angry he threatened to divorce her. Maxine held her position. He made good on his threat. He divorced Maxine for telling the truth.

McMillian knew Maxine was not telling the truth about sitting on his car talking to Georgette at the party that night. Why was McMillian so opposed to the prospect of my conviction being overturned?

No marriage built on real love should end that way. Could this marriage have been held together by something else? Did he have firsthand knowledge of or a possible role in this murder? Although this possibility didn't seem convincing enough for my lawyer and investigative team to pursue, I continued to dig.

I needed to continue searching until I became satisfied this wasn't just another dead end. I had no doubt Georgette and Foster were telling the truth about not seeing the prosecution's star witness, Maxine Bell, at the party. No one had! Were they hiding something? If not, why were their testimonies and statements to detective's contradictory regarding Sherese? There would come a time when I felt the need to speak with Georgette personally about these concerns.

I have absolutely nothing against Georgette. In fact, she has a special place in my heart. She stood up for me at trial when others kept quiet or told lies against me. I never believed Georgette was personally involved in the crime. But I needed to hear it from her own mouth.

I asked Andrea to contact Georgette and see if she would be willing to talk to me. Andrea left her a message. Eventually, Georgette replied she would love to talk to me and for me to please call her.

I was thinking maybe Georgette was finally willing to tell me more—maybe something she had not revealed to anyone else.

I called Georgette. She told me Sherese never got into their car that night and Sherese never left the party with them. But before we could delve deeper, she began telling me something far more significant than anything I had imagined.

My attorney, Adele Bernhard, wanted to retrieve my complete file from the police department in Suffolk County. She requested all documents under the Freedom of Information Act.

The police department denied our request. My attorney filed a lawsuit against them. The attorney that represents the police department agreed with us and informed the department it would need to turn the files over.

Among the files we received in the 2010s was a report about an individual whom detectives were covertly investigating. The name of this person was blacked out of the report sent to us:

> **On 7-7-75, the undersigned accompanied by Det. Arthur Hadel escorted ▮▮▮▮▮▮▮▮▮▮ of ▮▮▮▮▮▮▮▮▮ N.Y. into Mr. Richard Arthur, 57 West 57th Street, New York City, for purposes of a Polygraph examination.**
>
> **MR. ARTHUR conducted a Polygraph examination and upon completion stated that it was his opinion that ▮▮▮▮▮▮▮▮▮ was telling the truth. He further stated that he completely concurred with ▮▮▮▮▮▮▮ examination conducted on 5-1-75.**
>
> **Investigation continuing.**

The undersigned in this report was none other than detective Dennis Rafferty. But there was no other information that showed evidence of an investigation into this unknown person. Aside from the polygraph, the police files are silent on this issue.

Though most experts and courts regard polygraphs as faulty at best, this relevant information was swept under the rug and buried for over forty years. Police and the prosecution had no intention of allowing it to be brought before a jury as an element of this case. This person had been examined under the polygraph once, on May 1st. A decision was made to escort them to New York City for a second round.

The second test was conducted by the late Richard O. Arther, one of the leading authorities in the United States on polygraph testing in 1975. Arther arrived at the same conclusion as the less sophisticated examiner.

On May 8th, 1975, Rafferty wrote a statement for this individual to sign. Rafferty also signed as a witness. The signing of that statement made this individual more than just a suspect. The information he provided classified him as "a prime suspect."

The defense never even heard about it. It was only the recently granted FOI request that uncovered these details.

In May 2018, we finally received the information from the district attorney's office that detectives and the prosecution had concealed in 1975-76.

On May 9th, 1975, John W. Jones, Jr. notarized a statement taken by detective Rafferty. He waived his right to a lawyer and stated:

> **On Friday, Jan. 10, 1975, about 9:30 p.m. I went to a party on Bourdais Ave. N. Bellport NY. I left the party about 1:00 or 1:30 a.m., I was drunk. I didn't feel good. I went up the block and threw up. After throwing up, I cut through a dirt road to go home to my sister's house.**

> **While cutting, I tripped over a girl, I know it was a girl because of her hair and coat. I didn't recognize her at the time. I think when I tripped over her, I dropped my pick. It is black colored.**
>
> **After running away from the girl, I went home to my sister's. On May 9, 1975, I came to the Suffolk County Police Dept. Homicide Squad and was shown a photograph of where the girl I tripped over on January 11, 1975, was found.**
>
> **In the photograph, I saw a pick that looks just like the one I had on January 10, 1975. I also made a diagram showing how I left the party...**
>
> **This statement consisting of two pages had been read to me by Detective Dennis Rafferty, and I swear it is all true.**

This person put himself at the scene of the crime within the period of the actual murder. He admitted to dropping his own plastic pick at the scene. He went a step further and identified the pick as the same pick detectives showed him that was retrieved from the scene.

That's pertinent information!

When I first read the statement, I had some questions. The Jones statement was constructed strategically to work his story around the time frame the prosecutor used to point the finger at me. It implied that the Jones statement raised no contradictions to the prosecution's theory of the case.

There were other questions. There were about a hundred people who attended the party throughout the course of the night. There is not one person in his statement against whom to cross-reference anything Jones alleged.

When the defense presented its case, there were three witnesses who claimed they were in the same area where Sherese's body was found on Saturday evening and Sunday morning. All three claimed there was nobody there at the time.

Maude Hudson had testified she was the first to encounter the body. Something told her to touch it to see if Sherese was still alive. This witness touched her fur coat and found it completely dry. This also suggested Sherese may have been killed elsewhere and later dumped.

The prosecution had an opportunity to demolish the defense's position by calling the perfect witness, John Jones, to the witness stand. But he wasn't called. He was left untouched because the prosecutors didn't want the jury to know there was someone who put himself at the crime scene *and* left evidence.

The prosecutors could also have called the polygraph examiner to validate John Jones's story. But they weren't interested in disputing the defense's claim that the body was placed there. Why?

It was now obvious the prosecution didn't want the jury to consider any other person but me as the potential killer.

Jones tripped over the body, fell, and ran to his sister's house but never called the police to report the murder. If police had been notified closer to the time she'd been killed, they might have gathered enough evidence to easily solve the crime.

There is no clarity as to how Jones became of interest to the police. All that's known is that on April 18, 1975, he was arrested in Suffolk County for burglary. Less than two weeks later, he was questioned by detectives about this crime.

There was no reason for Jones to volunteer information about this case when he failed to do so at any time prior to his April arrest.

For some unspecified reason, Jones had no choice but to provide a story he hoped would justify his pick being at the crime scene without implicating himself in the crime.

Then there is the problem of Jones's route. He needed to travel southward to Brookhaven Avenue, to where he was staying that night. It does not make any sense to travel north to Hampton Avenue, walk all the way down to Mead Avenue, then cut through the Mead Avenue dirt road. There was no reason for Jones to use the dirt road where the body was found. His sister lived in the opposite direction. The explanation he gave was ridiculous!

To top it off, this guy never presented one alibi to support any of his story.

Why didn't they sample Jones's blood, hair, or fingernails?

A thorough investigation of this person should have been pursued. Throwing the case at me was the easier way out. They went so far as to manipulate the proceedings to conceal this information at a pretrial suppression hearing, then again at trial.

During the pretrial suppression hearing conducted on May 27th, 1975, the prosecution put detective Rafferty on the witness stand. He was questioned under oath by the prosecution and the defense about other suspects. The prosecution used Rafferty to establish that there were no other suspects considered in this case except those with criminal backgrounds. The prosecution misled the court and my defense attorney into believing there was no evidence that pointed to any other person besides me.

This pretrial hearing took place twenty-six days after Jones had given a statement to Rafferty placing himself at the crime scene dropping his black afro-pick at the crime scene right around the same time as the murder.

In my view, Rafferty committed perjury at that hearing. He—and the prosecution—knew another suspect was being investigated, and not because of "a bad criminal history."

As the police report clearly stated, that investigation was continuing.

On July 7th, 1975, detective Rafferty was one of the detectives who escorted John Jones to New York City for testing. He was also present during the polygraph recording. Jones was asked a total of four questions. The first three were:

1. Did you see Sherry Watson get choked to death?
2. Did you choke Sherry Watson to death?
3. Did you see Sherry Watson get hurt?

According to Arther, there were "slight indications of truthfulness" when Jones answered "no" to the above questions.

There were also "slight indications of truthfulness" when Jones answered "yes" to his fourth question:

4. Did you really stumble across Sherry Watson's body as you walked home?

How do slight indications of truthfulness translate into someone passing a lie detector test? To me, a slight indication does not sound convincing at all. It leaves room for doubt.

What's even worse about Arthur's opinion is that he attempts to validate his presumption of truthfulness. He administered and thus relied on his "known-solution peak-of-tension test."

Jones was asked, "Did you stab Sherry Watson in the back with a _____?" Inserted in the blank were seven different choices, only one of which was known to be true.

Jones replied "no" to each of the seven choices. On two separate tests, Jones did not react to the choice known to be true: "metal hair pick."

The very question asked by Arther's known-solution peak-of-tension test he determined as an additional indicator of truth.

According to an affidavit by renowned pathologist Michael M. Baden, the metal hair pick could not have caused the puncture wounds in this case. In an affidavit we submitted in our newly discovered evidence motion, Baden presented compelling insight and facts to back up his argument.

If there was any validity to the known-solution peak-of-tension test, it would have had no probative value as an indicator of truth based on the question asked.

Gerald Sullivan was the top district attorney in Suffolk County in 1975. He was assigned to the top cases and brought that county its highest conviction rate. He knew exactly what he was doing. Like detective Rafferty and his ruthless gang, ADA Sullivan was doing what he did best to secure a conviction with no concern for the possibility of innocence.

This was the same district attorney who emphasized in the presentencing report that "Deceased and family were above the normal class of people in Bellport area, she was educated and affable." He felt that "deceased murder was more serious than the death of an individual of a lesser social status in the community."

His biased remarks were disrespectful, and his actions showed a lack of concern about Sherese and her family. He concealed facts that sabotaged the prosecution, in violation of the law and the duties entrusted to him. At trial, in the presence of a jury, the prosecution failed to question detective Rafferty about other suspects. In fact, the prosecution used deception to protect Rafferty's knowledge about the "prime suspect" neither wanted the jury to know about.

The prosecution used false allegations and a deceptive tactical approach to divert my attorney's attention away from questions about other suspects.

During his questioning of Rafferty, my lawyer asked, "Officer, were there other suspects on the day you interviewed my client?"

The prosecution immediately objected and asked to approach the bench outside the presence of the jury. The jury was dismissed.

In part, the prosecution argued, "I'd like to take this opportunity to appraise counsel of something which he may not be aware of... he's opening the door if he proceeds with this line of questioning concerning suspects."

"There was a great deal of information from confidential informants, people who refused to come forward, but people who imparted this information who made Keith Bush a very definite suspect."

"There were at least several people who said the same thing that Maxine Bell said. These people have refused to come forward, and they have refused to have their names divulged. This information was known to investigating detectives and to some extent this witness."

"If counsel goes into the issue of other suspects, I am entitled to go into the issue on redirect of what made other people suspects as distinguished from Keith Bush."

"I think the witness would answer there was no other person connected to the crime by any evidence, and if any other person were suspects they were simply because of their bad criminal background… This is the door I assert counsel is opening."

The prosecution knew what Rafferty would say.

The defense was totally unaware of this hidden investigation. Having conceded to the prosecution's false contentions, my attorney addressed the court.

"I would look to your Honor for your consideration of his point. If I'm allowed to merely put forth this one question if there were other suspects, and if I do not go any further than that, I will not mention anybody's last name."

The prosecution knew his bluff was working. So, he said, "What I will do is object to the use of the word 'suspects' because that implies a conclusion on the part of the investigating police officers that there was suspicion as against other people, and the basis of that suspicion is what the jury is going to be concerned with."

The judge interjected.

"The question is whether you need use the word 'suspects' rather than—I understand what you're attempting to do and what

Mr. Seligman [my attorney] is attempting to do, and perhaps the solution to the dilemma might be the use of the word—or the use of the question, 'Were there any other persons under investigation?'"

The prosecution replied, "I don't object to that phrase, substituting the word for 'suspects,' but I wish to reserve my right to object to any matters inquired into as to why other person were under investigation."

The judge looked at my attorney. "You understand that you're skirting a very delicate area which is fraught with peril?"

My attorney answered, "I am making a statement for the record that my intention will be to merely ask the question as you purport."

The judge said, "I don't suggest—I suggested as of the use of the phrase. I don't tell you to use it. I don't suggest that you use the question."

My attorney responded, "My question to the court is if I will limit my examination on this point that were other people in this investigation and I go on to further subject matter and leave it, will you then allow Mr. Sullivan [the prosecutor] to go into it on redirect? I would not go any further than that mere question."

The prosecution countered, "My prior objection is to the relevancy of whether other persons were under investigation. That does not bear upon the case as against Keith Bush."

"I beg to differ with that," my attorney said.

The prosecution replied, "If counsel is attempting to show that there are other people that the jury must consider as possibly having done this crime simply because of the people that were under investigation is utterly inadmissible that is an incorrect inference, and I think I'm entitled to show at that point of any inference created or injected into the case why other people might have been under investigation and what distinguished them from Bush, I would ask counsel's purpose in doing that."

The judge: "Well, what he's done has been to apprise you of the area that you now tentatively are entering, and he need not have done that."

My attorney said, "I am stating to the court what I intend to ask this witness, and I would like a ruling from the court concerning—"

"What you're doing is asking for an advance ruling based on what has been stated on the record," the judge interjected, "and there's been no testimony on direct on this point, and you're going to have to use your own judgment. If you feel that it's appropriate, that is something for you to do. I can't suggest to you what you should or should not do."

"I'm not asking your Honor what I should or should not do," my attorney said. "I'm asking your Honor to give me a ruling that if I ask the question as we described, as we have discussed it and no further question on that point, will you then allow counsel to open the door on redirect concerning this issue?"

"He's entitled to ascertain who these people were and to develop that area," the judge replied.

At that point, the trial resumed in open court. My attorney never raised the question about other suspects.

The prosecution's sleight-of-hand manipulated the court and the defense into thinking no other suspects existed.

Controversy has always hung over polygraph testing. In 1975, some law enforcement agencies, prosecutors, and defense attorneys embraced it as if it was a hard science.

Even today, many in law enforcement venture into polygraph examination and hold that the testing is not flawed.

I have my doubts about polygraph examinations. But when my attorney, Bernhard, asked me in 2007 to take one, I agreed without hesitation.

I was given a polygraph examination on February 17th, 2008, by Mark Smith, a certified polygraph examiner and member of the American Psychological Association. He concluded, "Due to the lack of significant physiological reactions to the relevant questions, it is this examiner's opinion that he was *truthful* when he denied murdering Ms. Watson."

Smith also used the Objective Scoring System that determined my score of +33. Cutting scores for truthful charts are about +8 and higher. This put my score well over the range for truthful. The CPS II (another scoring measure) also put me over the range for truthful.

After I was tested, my lawyer told me that Smith was somewhat perplexed when he told her, "You know, this guy is really innocent."

Unfortunately, courts do not accept polygraph examinations. If the courts had accepted the polygraph results of John Jones, then they would have to accept mine. If polygraph testing was considered in court as valid, I would have immediately begged the mercy of the court that detective Rafferty and myself be subpoenaed and ordered to take one.

In 2018, when the defense first discovered the information and polygraph testing of John Jones, my attorney contacted Smith. We had some concerns about the language used by examiner Richard Arther, particularly his use of the phrase "slight indication of truthfulness" as a determination that John Jones was telling the truth.

According to Smith, Arther's slight indication of truthfulness, in 1975 was based on an antiquated system. He said that today these examinations are based on a number system, which is more accurate in determining truthfulness. Smith explained my number scores would not fall under the rubric of slight indication of truthfulness. My scores are much higher than John Jones's were when we both were asked and denied killing Sherese Watson.

There were obviously other suspects in this case. Detective Rafferty and the prosecution were fully aware of it. And the prosecution needed to keep that door closed.

The information John Jones provided to detectives, coupled with a fingerprint found at the crime scene that was hidden after it was discovered did not match me, was clearly exculpatory evidence in violation of *Brady v. Maryland*, 373 U.S. 83 (1963).

The prosecution also committed prosecutorial misconduct by refusing to hand this information over as required by law.

This is just one of many examples of foul play that led to the determination of that special commission in the late 1980s that there was evidence Suffolk County detectives and the district attorney's office were guilty of disturbing practices.

At trial, the defense's theory of the case pointed to Donald Crump, Larry Monroe, and Rawleigh Harris as the possible culprits.

The district attorney sought the assistance of Monroe and Harris to convince the jury that I was the only person the jury should consider as the perpetrator. Monroe and Harris were offered immunity in exchange for their testimony.

These three individuals went on to earn extensive criminal records after my conviction. Their records combined ran the gamut: Criminal possession of stolen property; unauthorized use of a vehicle; impersonation; possession of forged instrument; weapons charges; possession of burglary tools; criminal mischief; disorderly conduct; harassment; menacing; attempted and petit larceny; DUI; speed violations; aggravated and unlicensed driving; robberies and attempted robberies; possession and sales of controlled substances; burglaries; rape; sexual abuses, attempted and committed; and, of course, murder.

Donald Crump was protected by the prosecution for years. He was their informant. The other two were blessed with minimum sentences each time they were arrested, even for murder. The three became career criminals, though Crump never did state prison time.

There is an excellent chance two of these men are in the state and federal crime database. The last conviction of Monroe was for murder. He was given the minimum amount of time, a sentence of fifteen years to life. He was sentenced in May 1992 and would have been in the prison system when the crime DNA database was implemented for violent felony offenders. Harris's last release date from state prison after an attempted robbery from state prison was in September 2003; he would also be in the database.

Crump never did state prison time for the many crimes he committed because of his service as an informant for the district attorney's office. But his identical twin brother, Dennis Crump, did. Their crimes were as identical as their genes.

Like Donald, Dennis Crump also committed sex offenses as part of his criminal activities. Dennis was charged with rape in 1989 and pleaded to a reduced sexual misconduct charge. In 2004, Dennis was again charged with rape and unlawful imprisonment and was given a mere three-year prison term. Dennis also committed crimes such as attempted petit larceny, robbery, criminal trespassing/burglary, and menacing. His last release date from state prison was for assault in November 2008.

These crimes do not reflect, in any way, the multitude of crimes for which they were never caught.

After my conviction, we discovered three other people, aside from defense witness Nora Rush, who observed Sherese get into the infamous red car that night. These witnesses were Andre Smith, Darlene Rush, and Frank Turner.

There was already a lot of information pointing in the direction of the red car. We discovered even more.

The information Georgette Farmer gave me the night I talked with her on the phone was conveyed to her by a person named Nickey Hughley. He lost contact with her around the time of the murder and had found her years later on Facebook.

He asked her about what happened to her because she had disappeared. Georgette told him that after Sherese was killed she was traumatized, received counseling, and was sent away by her mother.

This opened the conversation about the murder. After Hughley told Farmer what he witnessed that night, Hughley told her to give me his phone number. I immediately contacted him.

He was from Center Moriches, a small town close to Bellport. He had a family who lived in Bellport. He came to town when he could to see his girlfriend, Georgette. Bellport also was the site of a lot of parties, which attracted people like Hughley from neighboring towns.

According to Hughley, he also attended the party the night Sherese was murdered. He doesn't remember the time, but thinks it was after midnight when he got to the party. He didn't stay long, nor did he go inside. He did not know Sherese.

While walking in the direction of his home, traveling down Brookhaven Avenue toward Mead Avenue, he observed a girl and a guy just ahead of him. He couldn't make out what they were saying but could hear them arguing about something.

They both stopped a little past the church, still arguing. The guy yelled at the girl (who he believes now was Sherese) and proceeded to go his own way, heading down Brookhaven Avenue in the opposite direction from the party.

He told me Sherese turned around, apparently upset, and walked toward him as if she was going back to the party.

As he was approaching, he saw two guys at the foundation of the church. He thinks Sherese may have been crying because the two guys were asking her if she was all right.

One of them put his arms around her, pretending to comfort her. They weren't being forceful but were trying to sweet-talk and lure her behind the foundation.

Hughley slowed down. One of the guys turned to face him and said, "Get the fuck out of here. Mind your fuckin' business!"

It was the Crump brothers. Hughley hesitated. He knew them from Riverhead. They had a reputation for making trouble and carrying guns.

He decided it was best to mind his own business.

He kept walking, even though he could hear the girl telling them things like, "No, stop, I want to go back to the party." As he walked away, he could hear them still trying to sweet-talk her.

Hughley told me about a few months after the murder, he got into a fight with someone else. The guy died from unrelated complications and Hughley was charged with manslaughter.

He ended up on the same tier with both Crump brothers in the county jail. One day, I was moved to that same tier. He said they had seen him when he tried to approach my cell. He was coming to tell me what he saw that night, and that the Crump brothers were on the tier. They saw him and immediately called him to the back. He was told to stay away from me. They didn't want Hughley near me because they knew he'd seen them that night.

I was moved off the tier in the morning the next day.

Hughley told me he ended up fighting both Crump brothers because they kept trying to intimidate him regarding what he saw that night.

In November 2017, Ike Maynes provided us with additional information about one of the Crump brothers.

According to Maynes, one day in 1975, he was with Raymond Hart at Shirley Trent's house on Horton Avenue in Riverhead, N.Y. He couldn't recall the date and time but did remember I was still in the county jail and had not yet been convicted.

The two were using Trent's garage to work on Hart's racecar. One of the Crump brothers came up the driveway and approached them with something heavy on his mind. Maynes didn't know which brother it was because they were identical twins.

He told them the guy they arrested from Bellport (me) didn't kill that girl (Sherese). He told them that "they" did it. He didn't say who "they" were but did say he couldn't sleep. It was really starting to bother him.

The Crump brother also said he went to the police to confess, but the police arrested him on other charges.

After the Crump brother left, Maynes told Hart people in Bellport knew I didn't do it. Rumors of guilt had already been circulating about Crump and some other guys from Riverhead.

I received a phone call at 6:53 p.m. on June 10th, 2018. The call came from brother Muhammad. His first word: "Peace."

I replied with the same greeting. Then he spoke again.

"Brother, that has been officially confirmed." Before I could reply, he continued. "I just got off the phone with my daughter."

His daughter had been wrestling with questions about her favorite uncle, Keith Taylor, ever since her father had told her what he knew.

Finally, she'd confronted someone in the family who was as close to her uncle as she was, his oldest son. His son confirmed that his father was the person who killed Sherese Watson. She immediately called her father to tell him he was right.

Muhammad's daughter was Taylor's favorite niece. She became a Black Israelite by way of his influence. She loved her uncle dearly and looked up to him.

Shortly after committing this murder, Taylor was committed to Brunswick, a mental institution in Amityville, N.Y. He was in and out of that hospital throughout the late 1970s and early 1980s.

Only the mother and the older family members knew about this family secret.

Muhammad strongly believes Taylor's closest cousin, Byrant Langhorne, is aware of Taylor's actions. Langhorne grew up in the 40th project in Queens. He and Taylor were like two "peas in a pod."

When Taylor and Langhorne were younger, they were always together. Langhorne later moved back to South Carolina, where he now lives around his extended family.

Taylor was deeply troubled for years. He lived his life in covert distress. Muhammad told me it was obvious Taylor was having problems dealing with what he had done. He lived his adult life in a deep depression for killing Sherese. Taylor used drugs to mask his pain. He used religion to help him fight his demons. He even once thought about coming forward, but of course didn't follow through.

Instead of addressing his sins by objectively accepting his fate before leaving this world, Taylor chose an easier way out. In 2008, when he could no longer deal with the weight of everything, Keith Taylor committed suicide by hanging himself.

Muhammad told me the Taylors are a close family. He believes it is hard even for good families to turn their loved ones over to the criminal justice system, for the rest of their lives.

He expressed hope that the possibility may now exist that someone from the family might be willing to talk about it. Keith

Taylor is no longer here. Exposing the truth could bring closure to everyone who suffered from this nightmare.

Muhammad's daughter, his first born, found it hard to accept the words of her own father about her favorite uncle that points to him as the sole individual responsible for the death of Sherese Watson.

These are the only directions to which the possible killer(s) have pointed in the forty-four years we have been searching.

One thing is for sure: the facts uncovered about John Jones move him above the boys in the red car on the list of possible suspects.

Who killed Sherese? I still don't know. DNA may be the only thing left that can tell us. One thing I do know, without a doubt, it was not me!

The Confession Takers

SUFFOLK COUNTY CONFESSION LIERS

Det. Dennis Rafferty

Det. August Stahl

Homicide detectives in shirts noting percent of cases in 1978 in which they obtained statements.

'All they need is a dead body and a confession... Everything is geared towards confessions and admission. They don't want to do the work on the hard cases... Henry O'Brian, former Suffolk district attorney.'

This chapter rides upon the painful memories of a harrowing journey that now binds me to so many others who have suffered at the hands of a flawed and biased system. In writing this chapter, I am reminded of my own struggles, my own battles against a system that sought to crush my spirit and deny me my humanity, intentionally!

As we navigate through the shadows of injustice illuminated by police misconduct, biased policies, flawed court decisions, and the shocking and growing number of exoneration cases across the country, we are confronted with the disturbing statistics and data that underscore the intentional abuse of that which has become ingrained within the justice system due to the lack of accountability laws, and of course, the question of racism.

Drawing upon the insights provided in the Suffolk County Conviction Integrity Bureau (CIB) investigation of my case, I will unravel the layers of racial hatred displayed by Detective August Stahl, underscoring the imperative need for retroactive accountability.

The revelations of racial hatred and systemic abuse unearthed by past and current investigative entities cut deep, piercing through the veneer of righteousness responsible for protecting our legal system. The words of detective August Stahl, dripping with venomous prejudice, echo in my mind, a stark reminder of the insidious nature of racism that continues to poison our society.

Detective August Stahl displayed evidence of racial hatred when questioned by the CIB. Four decades after detective Stahl participated in assaulting me, when asked if he remembered the Keith Bush case, this detective boldly stated: "Yeah, I know Keith

Bush, I remember. That fucking nigger did it, there is no doubt about it; he should have been executed for it."

In the same interview detective Stahl suggested the victim could have gotten the DNA, found under her fingernails, from anyone at what he described was "more like a riot" than a party. Suggesting the victim's alleged promiscuity renders the DNA question irrelevant.

Detective Stahl described homicide cases he worked in Amityville and Wyandanch (predominately black and poor communities) as "assaults or misdemeanor homicides." Again, totally disrespecting certain victims and the victim in this case.

When complimented on his looks for his age he response, "Yeah, but I can't pound people the way I used to be able to." Detective Stahl boldly responded when asked how hard he and the Homicide Division worked. He stated they did what they had to do to get the job done and that he would be indicted if he engaged in that conduct today."

It is also imperative to note when asked about additional suspects by the CIB the response given was, "Absolutely not." When mentioning the suspect by name and the details, detective Stahl remained adamant in his position and maintained it never happened.

Detective Stahl informed the CIB investigators that Detective Dennis Rafferty had alerted him about the inquiries into the Bush case. Detective Stahl asked the CIB investigators, "Why is this thing being opened again, I thought Tommy Spota took care of it?"

Detective Stahl articulated his response to CIB with no fear of consequences. Why should there be in the State of New York, where the pathway to justice will always be undermined by the lack of accountability. Detective August Stahl felt bold enough to say what he said because he was under the assumption that he was still protected by Suffolk's Blue Wall of Silence.

After all he has done to me and others in Suffolk County, he and detective Dennis Rafferty are probably still receiving the highest pensions in the country for the remainder of their lives. What a total disrespect to victims, exonerees, and the good people of Suffolk. To pay compensation to exonerees and continue to pay corrupt police who shamed Suffolk good name. Corruption in Suffolk went far beyond racism. Many of these cases led to several investigations in Suffolk and monetary damages from claims of police brutality and prosecutorial misconduct.

Marty Tankleff's, a Suffolk County exoneree, was a teenager arrested and convicted for the murder of his adoptive parents. The evidence used to convict him was an inconsistent coerced confession. The prosecution relied upon no physical evidence and an inconsistent confession to convict. Suffolk detective James McCready, the detective that took Marty confession was found to have committed perjury by a Commission in a 1985 murder trial. Three years before Marty's trial.

Former district attorney Tom *(**Tommy**)* Spota, set up roadblocks in the Tankleff case to obstruct his path to justice. The case garnered national attention and sparked discussions about the flaws in the justice system.

Tankleff's journey to exoneration was a testament to his resilience and the tireless efforts of advocates fighting to regain his freedom. The case serves as a cautionary tale about the dangers of unchecked power and the importance of holding authorities accountable for their actions. Former and current convicted district attorney Thomas Spota would play the same role in the Bush case that he played in the Marty Tankleff case.

In 2019, Spota got what was coming to him in a just way and ultimately open the pathway to my exoneration. He was convicted and sentenced to 5 years by the same County he had undermined for decades. Spota was found guilty of helping to cover for James Burke, Former Suffolk Police Chief with an ugly past of his own.

Burke was sentenced to just 46 months in federal prison for assaulting a handcuff suspect of stealing items including sex toys and child pornography from Burke police department SUV. He was also charged with obstruction of justice because his co-defendant Spota was trying to help him cover it up.

According to federal prosecutors investigating the Burke case, "Spota considered anyone cooperating with the investigation into Burke a "rat," demanded that a police officer find out who was cooperating and threatened that informant "would never work in Suffolk County again." Burke was released in 2019 and Spota was on his way to prison in 2019. Burke was arrested again for public lewdness, offering a sex act, and unlawful solicitation in 2023.

What does all of this have to do with the Bush case? These were the two departments blocking my efforts for decades. Spota and assistant district attorney Rosalind Grey literally roadblocked my case for over 10 years in my quest for justice during the time when DNA evidence excluded me. At one point it got so bad I was forced to sue the police department only to receive records of important information blacked out. Information I was totally unaware of.

For decades the truth was hidden in plain sight and its secret protected by police and prosecutors throughout the years. Like

Spota some of these prosecutions had moved up in ranks now serving as Justices of the court.

In 2019, my attorney Adele Barnhard, had reconstructed her legal strategic approach and exposed the flaws in the state case down to its details. For the first time, witnesses were coming forward, expert witnesses today, destroying trial expert witnesses' testimony and the physical evidence presented at trial.

The fall of Spota came at the perfect time. It led to the appointment of Tim Sini, the new Chief District Attorney with promises of cleaning up Suffolk County. The CIB was implemented. What was held in darkness for 44 years came to light. But justice did not come alone. The people of righteousness came with it.

Examples of injustice serve as powerful reminders of the human cost of systemic failures in the criminal justice system. Exonerees endured years of wrongful imprisonment, facing unimaginable challenges. Some exonerees have not been compensated for their enslavement in States with no reparatory laws. These cases highlight the need for comprehensive reform and accountability to prevent future miscarriages of justice.

The "Blue Wall of Silence" also provides factual evidence of abuse that is of critical importance as to why America needs to dismantle this culture of complicity to pave the way for genuine accountability and reform. By shedding light on the consequences of turning a blind eye to injustice, we confront the stark reality that those who choose not to confront intentional misconduct or criminal activities are complicit in perpetuating it.

An African American woman who worked as a secretary for the prosecution in this case approached my mother outside the court room in 1975. According to this woman, "she was not at the liberty of discussing the details of the case" but wanted my mother to believe in what I was telling her. She just wanted to encourage my mother to never stop fighting.

Obviously, this woman wanted badly to reveal something of significance but instead bowed to the blue wall of silence. Four decades later, as it turns out, this information was strong enough to overturn my conviction had it been revealed at that time. I would not have spent over 44 years in captivity. The prevailing question stands.

Where is the protection against a code of silence when it involves the moral responsibility to protect the rights of others, especially minors? What human being would let corrupt police send an innocent boy to prison with a death sentence when that person knew the police intentionally hid information that could prove that person's innocence?

The silence of those who turn a blind eye to injustice are the actors in concert to the very injustice their silence serves. Protecting injustice at all costs is something that should weigh heavily on the advocacy of democracy. It should be more like a burden that America could not bear to ignore. It is a call to action, a plea for accountability, and a demand for reform that resonates deep within my being.

The blue wall of silence also referred to as (Blue Code or Blue Shield), must meet its collision course with accountability and reform. Whistleblowers who lean on justice over injustice should not be retaliated against by the same people that have sworn to protect justice. Major contradictions of this nature require national discussion for change.

In Suffolk County, there is clear evidence of retaliation by Suffolk police against whistleblowers who stand on the side of justice. In every case that person would pay a price. This includes a setting Justice of the court.

Exoneration cases continue to raise serious questions about the lack of a constitutional protection clause against fear of retaliation for disclosure of intentional violation of a minor's constitutional rights over law enforcement code of silence.

Today's overwhelming evidence of injustice can be traced directly to video recordings of police brutality and murders, bias policies, court decisions and exoneration cases around the country. Statistics and other relevant data also give substance to these concerns still present in the justice system.

Just about every exoneration case in the country has a common link to the nationwide practice of how police and district attorneys investigate and prosecute cases. Some of these common factors in wrongful convictions are eyewitness misidentification, false confessions, flawed forensic evidence, perjured testimony, and police/prosecutorial misconduct (tampering/falsifying evidence, intimidating witnesses, etc.).

The statistics and data presented in this book paint a grim picture of a system rife with bias, corruption, and unchecked power. The stories of wrongful convictions and shattered lives serve as a sad reminder of the human cost of institutional failures and moral compromises.

On January 14, 1975, the morning of my arrest I immediate made claims of police brutality. The complaints made by me against the police would not come to light for many years even after several cases that would become the focus in several studies investigating brutality and misconduct in Suffolk County.

During this same period, during the 1970s and 1980s, just about all of Suffolk County convictions involved confessions. Hundreds of them were routinely being introduced into evidence and over 95% of them resulting in conviction. Many of these convictions relied upon circumstantial evidence and/or just a confession.

The New York State Court of Appeals reversed numerous cases for improperly obtaining confessions in Suffolk. In my case, the courts were only willing to go as far as to acknowledge my presence at the precinct as "the result of police deception and trickery." But the courts would not go any further even though the prosecution star witness recanted at my probable cause hearing.

In a Suffolk County Newsday study, from 1970 to 1980, a gang of corrupt detectives wore t-shirts bragging about a 97% confession rate in murder cases. Ninety-seven percent! That's insane. Far exceedingly any other county in the nation this ridiculously high percentage of conviction rates based solely upon confession had sent shock waves around the nation and earned Suffolk police the nickname: The Confession Takers!

Suffolk County would become the subject of a wide amount of notoriety for its abuse of power. In time, law enforcement and the district attorney office would be highly criticized by criminal justice experts around the country. In 1979, the National Law Journal, and in 1980, the Suffolk County Bar Association blast Suffolk police with strong language of police brutality in coercion of confessions with language of deep concern.

The National Law Journal 1979 article described allegations of abuse that noted "a similarity in the typed of torture allegedly employed: being administered by telephone books used as a cushion to avoid leaving telltale bruises, blackjacks used on the sole of the feet and other sensitive areas, kicks, and punches to the genitals."

In 1985, Suffolk County paid out 80,000.00 in a settlement involving a 17- year-old teen. In 1981, William Rupp was awarded monetary damages when a jury determined Suffolk police coerced a confession later proven to be false. Stories of similar complaints as Rupp by other defendants many of these complaints were identical complaints made by me, i.e., beaten with fist or telephone books on top of head to leave no mark and testicle assault.

In my case, five months after I was abused, tortured, and arrested, the police and the prosecution would intentionally do something else just as outrageous to me as they did when they assaulted me and violated my constitutional rights. It would cost me over 44 years of my life to triumphant over injustice.

My case occurred within the time frame of these studies, reports, and articles, interestingly, my case was never cited. Court of Appeals reversals of about 10 major murder cases were for the same reasons relative to my case, the courts acknowledgement of a serious problem with the confessions by Suffolk Police.

In many of these cases I have already made similar claims. Worse than that, the detectives responsible for violating those other defendants' constitutional rights were the same detectives who violated my constitutional rights. These same detectives led to many of Suffolk cases being reversed based on improper confessions and would ultimately become the same detective that sparked an investigation of Suffolk police and the district attorney office.

Detective Dennis Rafferty, the main detective in my case, not only played the most significant role in assaulting me and concealed vital evidence, but this is also the very detective that sparked the hold investigation of Suffolk County Law Enforcement abuse. His name was mentioned in several publicized murder cases.

The climate of abuse by Suffolk police and the district attorney office led to a special request by Supreme Court Justice Stuart Namm to the late New York State Governor Mario M. Cuomo. That Commission was granted based on two murder trial Justice Namm resided over and an attempt by Suffolk police to intimidate a setting justice of the court.

Consistent with other fact-finding conclusion, the New York State Investigation Commission determined that Suffolk County police and the district attorney office engaged in misconduct, mismanagement in investigations and prosecutions, over-reliance on confessions at an astonishingly high rate, perjury, credibility problems with prosecution witnesses, grave improprieties in narcotics operation, drug use by narcotic officers, illegal wiretaps, unreliable informant testimony, fraud, and favoritism, etc.

In the highly publicized Diaz murder confession case, detective Rafferty conspired with other detectives to do the same exact thing he did in my case. Detectives fabricated a confession of lies that was later found to be untrue. In my conviction, Suffolk Police tricked and deceived me, placed me incommunicado, mentally confused, and physically gang assaulted me into signing a confession I never read or admitted to.

Justice Namm took a stand against injustice. He would pay the price by being labelled a whistleblower just for standing on the right side of justice. He would not be re-elected for doing so. Justice Namm returned to the South where he wrote the book, "A Whistleblower's Lament: The Perverted Pursuit of Justice in the State of New York." Why must one pay such a heavy price just for protecting justice or for standing against injustice?

Thomas Spota has a history in Suffolk judiciary that goes back to 1975, the time of my arrest. Spota and Gerald Sullivan (the district attorney that prosecuted my case) were both district attorneys at that time. It was Spota who talked Sullivan into leaving the district attorney office for a switch in private practice.

Spota and Sullivan joined forces with a team of attorneys and formulated their own private practice of a defense dream teams that maintained their tied to the district attorney office while representing high profile individuals like politicians, polices, judges, etc. The history of that relationship consists of another chapter of foul play consistent with but not directly tied to my case. Crooked police and unjust district attorneys violating the rights of its teens under the protection of a governmental system had cursed the good people of Suffolk with a shameful past. The courageous and righteous fortitude of the Suffolk people demanding the need for change is the only way for Suffolk to restore its good name.

These two issues most resides at the heart of this argument or criminal justice abuse will continue to go unpunished and swept under the rug while the Constitution and the American principle of democracy will continue to be disrespected by the very people selling this conceptual theory to the world.

In the silence of the night for many years confined to a cage, I have reflected on the atrocities I have suffered at the hands of a flawed system, I am scared with a sense of urgency and purpose. This is not just a document; it is a testament to my commitment to stand up for what is right, to speak out against injustice, and to advocate for a future where justice is not a distant dream but a tangible reality for all.

As I pen these words with a heavy heart and a determined spirit, I invite you to join me on this journey of introspection, empathy, and action. Let us be the voices of change, the champions of justice, and the architects of a more equitable and compassionate society. Together, we can rewrite the narrative of our legal system, infusing it with the values of fairness, integrity, and humanity that define the true essence of justice.

Through the lens of my eyes and the broader context of criminal justice abuse, this case underscores the urgent need for reform and an accountability law to sustain it coupled with a national "Mandatory Reparatory Compensation Law" for all wrongfully convicted individuals. It emphasizes that without robust accountability laws at the national or state level, the cycle of criminal justice abuse will persist unchecked, undermining the very principles of democracy and constitutional rights that has failed to form the bedrock of American society.

In essence, this case, serves as a clarion call to action, urging us to confront the uncomfortable truths embedded within the American legal system and to strive towards a future where justice is not a privilege but a fundamental right for all individuals, irrespective of race or background.

Recommendations for reform include increased oversight of law enforcement practices, enhanced training on interrogation techniques, and the establishment of independent review boards to investigate claims of misconduct. By addressing the root causes of corruption and abuse in the criminal justice system, Suffolk County can begin to rebuild trust with its residents and uphold the principles of justice and fairness for all.

Detective Stahl's audacity in making reprehensible statements reflects a deeper malaise within the system—a culture of impunity fostered by the veil of silence that shrouds misconduct and shields wrongdoers from facing the repercussions of their actions. The fact that individuals like Detectives August Stahl and Dennis Rafferty, who have caused me immeasurable harm, continue to receive the highest pensions in the country is a stark reminder of the systemic failures that perpetuate injustice.

It is a travesty of justice, a betrayal of trust, and a total disrespect to the victims, exonerees, and the community at large to witness corrupt individuals being rewarded while those they have wronged are left to pick up the pieces of shattered lives. The very notion that individuals who have brought shame and suffering upon the principles of democracy are being compensated while exonerees struggle to rebuild their lives is a profound injustice that cannot be ignored.

The absence of accountability not only allowed individuals like Detective Stahl to reign in terror but also perpetuated a cycle of abuse and impunity that erodes the very fabric of our society. It is a stain on the moral conscience of Suffolk County and a betrayal of the principles of justice and fairness that should underpin our legal system.

As I grapple with the implications of this systemic failure, I am reminded of the urgent need for reform, for a reckoning with the past, and for a commitment to ensuring that those who abuse their power are held accountable for their actions. It is only through a collective effort to demand transparency, accountability, and justice that we can begin to dismantle the structures of oppression and create a more equitable and compassionate society for all.

These boldacious and outrageous statements made by detective Stahl was a direct slap in the face to the Black community and the American principles of democracy. This type of thinking continues to go unchallenged because America still has no checks and balance in its legal system. Without reparation and accountability laws applied to every exoneration case in America there can be no real justice. Only a blessing from God and courage from the righteous working to reform the legal system drowning in its own contradictions.

As I embark on this journey of introspection and advocacy for change, I invite you to walk alongside me, to lend your ears and raise your voice to the chorus of those who refuse to be silenced, who refuse to accept injustice as the status quo. Together, let us be the agents of change, the architects of a more just and equitable society, where the shadows of injustice are banished, and the light of truth and fairness shines bright for all to see.

Privileged Status Over Accountability

Thomas Spota
District Attorney

District Attorney
Gerald Sullivan

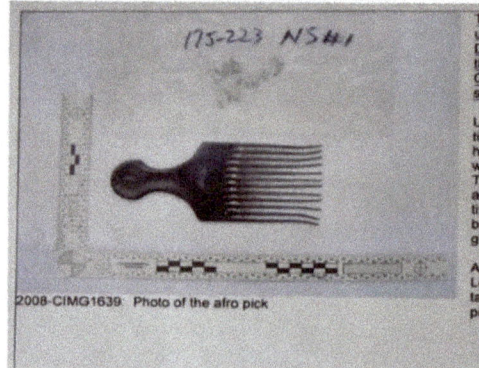

2008-CIMG1639 Photo of the afro pick

The afro pick was packaged in an unsigned/unsealed clear plastic bag. Documents indicate that it was recovered near the victim's body. According to ADA Rosalind Gray, this item was in the DA's file and not stored with the remainder of the evidence.

Upon examination, it was determined that the tines of the afro pick are probably too flimsy to have produced the wounds to the victim's back, which is in line with the original assessment. The only foreseeable way is if the tines were at an acute angle to the skin, thus limiting the tines' ability to flex. It was also noted that the brown material near the base of the tines is granular, like sand.

A discussion ensued between Mr. Galdi, Ms. Lee-Wyss, and myself as to what samples to take from the afro pick. It was agreed by those present that three samples were to be taken:
#1   Swab of the handle
#2   Swab of the base of tines
#3   Swab of the tines

In the United States, "No person can put himself above the law of the constitution. That's why Americans can say, ours is a government of laws, not of men." <u>Marbury vs. Madison</u>, 1 Cranch 137, 163 (1803). Is America drowning in her own contradictions?

This book is the story of two victims whose victimhood was intertwined: Sherese Watson and me. We both were arguably doubly victimized.

Sherese was, of course, first the victim of a cruel and senseless murder. But after that, the search for her true killer was abandoned in favor of an easier target. I became the scapegoat—a stand-in for the truth because the truth would have taken more time and effort to pursue.

I became a victim when I was sacrificed on this alter of expediency through police and prosecutorial tactics that hinged on coercion, concealment, and sleight-of-hand. I was also victimized a second time by a system that repeatedly refused to entertain my consistent claims of innocence, even punishing me for being principled and honest.

None of these instances of victimization were accidental or natural. Sherese didn't die from an illness; I wasn't confined by a clerical error. All these acts were carried out by individual people making individual decisions. There were dozens of people who played some role in this case over the decades. Some no doubt made honest mistakes or acted as best they could with the limited information available to them. But some clearly did have access to the broader picture and still chose to act in ways that perpetuated this farcical miscarriage of justice.

What droves these actors? Hatred? Ignorance? Racism? Disinterest? Laziness? Was it a desire to cover their own asses? Perhaps it was a combination of these factors. I can't look into their minds to uncover their deepest motivations. Whatever the reasons, though, they failed to do the jobs that they were entrusted to do.

Instead, they violated constitutional and legal principles, as well as simple human decency.

We should not forget that the foremost perpetrator in this debacle is the unnamed person, possibly John W. Jones, Jr., who killed Watson. It was that act that launched all others. It was the crime that spawned new crimes.

If not, John W. Jones, whoever killed Sherese still deserves to be held accountable for their heinous act. Unfortunately, we will probably never know for certain who did it. Even if we could say it was John W. Jones that person is also dead now, beyond any accountability the law could provide.

What's infuriating, though, is that we might have known. We might have held the right person accountable. There were leads; there was evidence. It was because of the decisions to relentlessly pin me to the murder to the exclusion of other possibilities—even when the case against me was flimsy and countervailing facts were glaringly apparent—that justice for Sherese has still not been obtained, and new injustices were allowed to pile up.

Some of those who carried out these unjust acts are beyond legal accountability themselves now, having gone to their graves over the intervening forty-four years from arrest to exoneration. The only corrective action available is making the hard truth known that their names are tied to these sorry decisions.

Yet others tied to this case are still around. Some are resting comfortably in retirement, collecting taxpayer-funded pensions. A few even remain active in government.

In its investigation and other documents, the Suffolk County District Attorney's Integrity Unit has agreed that many of the actions taken by members of the police and the broader justice system were wrong. Still, no charges have been brought against the actors; no lawsuits; no job dismissals; no consequences at all. The county, the state, and even the federal government have paid millions of dollars, first to cause the damage it did to me and my family, then to "repair" it. But if there is no attempt to hold bad actors accountable within the system, then all this taxpayer money amounts to nothing more than an insurance payout—the cost of doing business with corrupt individuals.

As the Long Island newspaper *Newsday* reported after my exoneration, several people had access to evidence pointing away from Bush that was withheld, including detectives Dennis Rafferty, August Stahl, and prosecutor Gerald Sullivan.

"Over the past four decades, various Suffolk police and prosecutors had access to my homicide files containing incriminating documents about the other potential suspect, John W. Jones Jr. Yet this evidence remained unknown publicly until disclosed just months prior to my exoneration in May 2019," the paper wrote in one article.

Others who would have had the ability to access the files and see for themselves that the case didn't hold up include former Suffolk District Attorney Thomas Spota, whose office repeatedly pushed back against my attempts to get my case looked at again; Suffolk County Judge Paul Hensley and Suffolk County Supreme Court Justice John B. Collins, who both served as assistant district attorneys in Suffolk county; other police officers connected to the case over the years; and numerous prosecutors. Notably, prosecutor Rosalind C. Gray, who is currently at the district attorney's office, was responsible for working on the several attempts by me to test DNA from the scene of the crime, including from the black plastic comb. Though the documents about Jones would have been available, none was brought up in court.

Retired State Supreme Court Justice Martin I. Efman, who presided over the DNA hearings, told *Newsday* in an interview he was "surprised" that the Jones documents were never revealed. "I don't know how it could not have been found," he said.

Hensley, for his part, approved a Freedom of Information Law request I made in 1989 for my entire case file. Somehow, the exculpatory files, including those implicating Jones, were absent from the tranche of documents released—though we know now that they definitively existed at the time.

This decision to hide exculpatory evidence, perpetrated first in the 1970s, was repeated by a new generation of officials in the late 1980s. Had they been included, perhaps my exoneration would have come twenty years earlier than it did. The investigation into Sherese's murder might also have been salvageable given that many of the players would still have been alive.

During the CIB's investigation, Rafferty acknowledged that he took Jones' statement in 1975 and accompanied Jones for a lie detector test. He and others in the police department understood there were other credible suspects in this case from the very beginning.

The answer is racism. These officers didn't care if they ruined my life, my family, Sherese's family, the friends, and neighbors touched by the crime, or the Black community in this enclave of Long Island. They cared only about clearing cases by whatever means necessary—about making their numbers look good. If innocent people had to suffer to get another case off their books, so be it.

It's apparent that the "racial animus" that fueled the department's discarding of life to reach an institutional goal extends beyond me alone. In its court filing in favor of my exoneration, the district attorney's office makes clear that the investigation into Watson's murder was cursory at best.

"The Suffolk Homicide Detectives relied on a coerced confession. They short-circuited the investigation. They discarded and disregarded other evidence that would have helped to solve the crime. For example, there may have been an actual rape. However, my defense had been unable to discover whether the Suffolk County medical examiner's office examined the deceased with that issue in mind or even whether a rape kit was prepared.

"For all we know, there may still be biological material in a rape kit somewhere. The deceased may have been killed someplace else and moved to the field behind the church, a point some of the witnesses tried to make at the trial when they testified that a day prior to the body's discovery, the body had not been in the location where it was found. The small wounds on the decedent's back and side might have been caused by something other than a comb. Once the police obtained the confession, all further investigation ceased."

The misdeeds surrounding Sherese and myself were not limited to omissions and coverups, either. They went beyond neglect to the purposeful invention of evidence. Detective Severino, a serologist from the Suffolk County Crime Laboratory, who testified in 1976 that cloth fibers observed in the material removed from beneath Watson's fingernails were like cloth fibers in my jacket, greatly exaggerated the quality of the evidence.

"It is now painfully obvious that Detective Severino's testimony was flawed and unscientific," explains the motion to exonerate me. First, his approach was biased. Instead of investigating broadly and considering what information the fibers found under the victim's fingernails might reveal about her death or about the perpetrator(s), Severino used the information to build a case against me exclusively. He compared what he found in the fingernail scrapings only to articles of my clothing. He failed to compare the fibers found in the scrapings to the fibers of the victim's clothing or to anyone else's clothing.

Second, the Detective's statements of probability were improper, unscientific, and were used to point the target at me. At the trial, he opined that, 'The chances of having three fibers present on fingernail scrapings that are like one article of clothing are very, very remote. Therefore, the fingernail scrapings did contain fibers from the defendant's jacket.'"

"There is no basis for his statement. It is completely improper to make a statement of probability when there is no database upon which to rely. All detective Severino should have said was, 'the fibers in the scrapings were similar in color and composition to the fibers in the jacket.' Without a database of fibers with which to refer, it is impossible to estimate how rare or frequent the presence of any fibers might be."

Today, of course, we have the DNA evidence from under Sherese's fingernails that excludes me. That hard-won evidence directly contradicts Severino's assertions. He wouldn't have had access to such DNA testing at the time. Nevertheless, it calls his testimony—and the efforts he made to conduct an impartial, scientific analysis—into serious doubt. As the motion explains,

Severino "overstated the probative value of fiber evidence the state used to link me to the murder. Severino's conclusion lacked any scientific support whatsoever and was an impermissible and material overstatement. It was impossible for him to conclude that the fibers came from any item of clothing."

Severino wasn't the only expert who overstated his case. There was also the testimony from Dr. Adelman, the deputy chief medical examiner, who claimed that the metal afro pick tied me to the murder—despite the fact that a different, plastic comb was found at the crime scene. For some reason, he chose to ignore the actual object that accompanied the murder.

Even more galling is that Adelman lent his credibility to the idea that the metal tines of the comb were consistent with the puncture wounds on Sherese's body when no actual measurements were even done to compare them. No measurements even needed to be done, though, to determine that it would have been physically impossible to stab someone with a multi-pronged metal object and produce single-puncture wounds. When you stick a fork deep enough into a piece of meat, all the tines must go in—they're inseparable. You don't have to be an expert to recognize this fact.

Yet somehow Adelman apparently didn't recognize it and argued that the wounds "were consistent with the front three prongs" of the ten-pronged metal pick, and that the "distances appear to be consistent."

In a subsequent review prior to my exoneration, pathologist Dr. Michael Baden reviewed the autopsy report, the confession, the autopsy photographs, a photograph of the comb, and Adelman's testimony.

Baden said that the ten-pronged afro-pick comb retrieved from my home could not have inflicted the wounds on the victim's back: "First, the puncture wounds are clustered in groups of threes and are close together, inconsistent with the spaces between the comb prongs; other wounds are single punctures. Further, it would have been impossible for a single prong of the comb to penetrate more deeply than the other prongs, but the autopsy report records a single puncture penetrating to a depth of 1-1/4 inches into the peritoneal cavity."

Lie on top of lie on top of lie was what put me in prison and kept me there for so long. There were opportunities at every juncture for those in control of my fate to do the right thing—to at least entertain the possibility that I might be telling the truth.

Instead, officials went down the opposite path, making every effort to ensure that the truth could not emerge. Sometimes this involved wanton stonewalling, simply ignoring his pleas. At other times, it involved sinister acts.

Perhaps the most sinister was the destruction of that pick—the supposed murder weapon. In 1983, someone—we will never know who—opened the box of evidence in my case, removing and destroying the pick. They did not sign their name when they removed the box from evidence.

Only a limited number of people from the district attorney's office would have had both the opportunity and motive to commit such an act. Whoever they were, they knew way back then that the story the police and prosecutors had told could not stand up to the stark reality of the facts. They must have wanted to make sure that the truth of this horrible miscarriage of justice never could come out.

Yet the facts have a stubborn habit of asserting themselves, no matter how much some of us may wish it to be otherwise. Real criminals get away with their crimes—until they don't. Whoever tried to bury the truth of Sherese Watson's murder and Keith Bush's conviction couldn't cover everything and everyone up forever. The coercive confession mill of the Suffolk County police was eventually exposed and shown to produce untrustworthy results. Maxine Bell eventually recanted her testimony. Later experts reassessed former ones. Someone places himself at the crime scene. DNA testing emerged, unraveling the fantasy spun by an earlier generation of criminal justice officials.

Although the destroyed pick couldn't be tested anymore, there was plenty of evidence still to go over. Though the district attorney's office at the time fought at every juncture to prevent the testing of fingernail scrapings and other materials, it could not disobey the appellate division, which saw through this tactic and ordered further testing. As the appellate decision said, "Given the sample of genetic material recovered from the fingernail scrapings already tested and the sample of genetic material recovered from the black plastic comb found at the scene, the County Court should have determined that a reasonable probability existed of a more favorable verdict if further testing was conducted on the previously untested fingernail scrapings and showed that the male contributor to these two prior samples shared a common source and did not come from the defendant."

This DNA testing was imperative in sowing some of the seeds of doubt that eventually toppled my conviction. My DNA did not appear anywhere. I simply could not be connected to the victim or to the crime scene. And none of Sherese's genetic material was found on me or on my clothing. At arrest, police scrutinized my fingernails. Colored fibers were found under my nails, but "microscopic comparison of these fibers against the victim's clothing failed to reveal any similarities" to the victim's clothing. No traces of the victim's biology were found under my nails—even though I supposedly strangled her just two days earlier.

As the motion in the exoneration noted, "The clothing Bush wore to the party was taken from his home immediately after his arrest and only three days after the victim disappeared. Examination of Bush's jacket, basketball shirt, chinos, and sneakers revealed no traces of the deceased's blood—even though the deceased's side and back were covered in wounds and there was blood on her clothing. There was no trace of the victim's biology on Bush and no trace of Bush's biology on the victim."

This is not to say that no DNA was found; there is indeed evidence that someone was at the crime scene. Without being able to test it against other possible suspects, we may never know to whom that DNA belongs. We may have the molecular identity of the killer, just not the name. What we can say with absolute confidence, though, is that it does not belong to me. Why have so many people who worked on this case made decisions that exacerbated the injustice of it? That's a difficult—and likely multifaceted—question. It seems probable from the information we do have that some of the motivations had little to do with me. on a personal level. This was not a conspiracy against one man. There are patterns like this case in other cases, with forced confessions, botched and destroyed evidence, and refusals to pursue avenues that might uncover inconvenient truths.

No, this was a conspiracy *for* the preservation of power, prestige, control. Neither Sherese, I, nor anyone else in its way were merely trampled over.

That is why it is so important that those who participated be named, shamed, and—where possible—held accountable. If we don't reckon with those who subvert freedom and justice, we leave ourselves open to further abuses. It has happened before. When a nation places privileged status over accountability, you can be sure that it will happen again and again and again.

Exoneration

Justice is not won by the statues of law. Justice is won by "Righteous Minds" with the courage to defend what is just in support of the statues of law.

My attorney Adele Bernhard and the Innocent Project students are working on my case.

Former District Attorney Tim Sini and Conviction Integrity Bureau staff discussing my case. Mr. Sini was not re-elected for his attempt at rooting out corruption in Suffolk County.

Unshackling the Truth: Triumphant Over Injustice

I first met Keith when he and I were working together on the docks for a trucking company in Bridgeport, CT. I was working nights and going to school for journalism at the time. Over months of conversations, I found out that he had formerly been a convict, and he found out that I was a writer.

I had no idea at first about the gravity—or the injustice—of his case. I knew that he maintained his innocence, but I (being a naïve White boy from the suburbs) had no way to tell whether that was just something lots of former prisoners said.

It hardly mattered to me what had happened in his past, though. He was one of the friendliest and most thoughtful people I had met at that job. It's astounding to me now that the years of abuse he suffered through the police, the prisons, and the justice system led him to become one of the most fully *human* people I've ever met. As he's said himself, things could easily have gone much differently for him.

Keith had mentioned to me a few times that he was working on a story about his experiences, and eventually gave me the draft of what he'd written up to that point.

After reading through the first few chapters, I realized that what he had been through went beyond anything I'd imagined. I also quickly came to understand that he wasn't just *saying* he was innocent—he'd been making herculean efforts to prove it his entire adult life.

Keith had no compunction about providing more details for anything I asked about or for giving me access to the mountain of documents that accumulated around his case over the years. It was as much because of his genuine forthrightness that I was convinced of his innocence as it was any of the facts of the case (though those alone were enough to demonstrate that he was a victim, not a perpetrator, many times over).

Keith's case still appeared to be spinning its wheels. He was consistently pursuing multiple avenues to break the chains that continued to drag at his heels. But years of dead ends had made him justifiably skeptical that he would ever get a fair shot at exoneration. Writing a book was perhaps the only way the truth could be told.

Little did we know that after forty-four years, the stars were finally beginning to align, and God would send him some angles.

After Keith's team filed its Freedom of Information requests and information about the cover-up of John J. Jones surfaced, events moved quickly.

One day in 2018, Keith came to me with copies of the redacted July 1975 detective's report filed by Rafferty in which an unidentified individual was said to have been taken to New York City for a polygraph test.

"They covered this up," he told me point-blank.

Even as his legal team was attempting to uncover more information about it, Keith was ready to go into the city and find the location of the now-defunct polygraph institute to see if he could uncover any more information himself.

That is the nature of his perseverance.

It wasn't just that new evidence of obfuscation and corruption on the part of the Suffolk Country Police and the district attorney's office were being unveiled, though.

In the last decade, New York has been at the forefront in launching several "integrity" programs to combat corruption, protect taxpayer dollars, and right old wrongs. One of those units—the Suffolk County Conviction Integrity Bureau—was created in 2018 by District Attorney Timothy Sini for the express purpose of reviewing cases like Keith's. It was perhaps by coincidence that compelling new evidence was coming to light just as this effort was being launched.

There's little doubt that Sini's Integrity Bureau played a pivotal role in finally restoring Keith's good name. It marked a change in culture in the justice system on Long Island that encouraged investigators to question the judgment of their own department (or at least the earlier judgments of the department's former occupants).

It's not unusual for the culture of an organization or a society to take a long time to change. Indeed, it often only happens through the drip-drip process of attrition, as old names drop out and new ones take their place.

After all, it's not as if it was a secret that corruption, racism, and other shady practices had infected parts of the Long Island justice system. Rafferty was exposed as a purveyor of forced confessions a generation ago. Periodic scandals about police procedures bubbled up throughout the 80s, 90s, and into the early 2000s.

It wasn't even that long ago that former Suffolk district attorney Thomas Spota was blocking any action on Keith's case, even after the DNA evidence had raised serious doubts. Now Spota himself has been convicted of federal charges for allegedly covering up criminal activities by former Suffolk Police Chief of Department James Burke.

Burke himself was sentenced to forty-six months in prison after being convicted of beating a Smithtown man who broke into

Burke's Suffolk County Police Department-issued SUV in 2012. Burke was found to have obstructed the federal civil rights investigation into that assault.

In an ironic twist, Spota's head of the anti-corruption bureau, Christopher McPartland, was indicted along with him on charges of obstructing the FBI investigation that led to Burke's conviction.

It was just one more example of the abuse of power that has been rampant for decades.

The timing was again fortuitous: Spota resigned in 2017 as the indictment against him came down, leaving Keith's appeals for justice to be viewed by fresh eyes.

It was the culmination of all these factors and more that led Howard S. Master, the man appointed by Sini to oversee wrongful conviction claims, to enter the fray.

Master conducted his own investigation into Keith's case, reviewing the decades of trials, appeals, and revelations. He even retested samples for DNA. In reviewing what appeared to be serious oversights (if not straight-up corruption) in failing to provide the evidence surrounding Jones, Master told *Newsday*, "To the extent that there was perjury or misstatements—and I'm not saying there was, I don't know yet—but if there was, that obviously would factor into a determination of whether it makes sense to vacate his [Keith's] conviction."

Master's work on the case lasted for nearly a year. When it was concluded, he determined that Bush had been right all along.

The district attorney's office did an about-face: after decades of vehement opposition to every move Keith made, the office now decided to back him entirely. The DA joined Keith's team, filing a motion in support of Keith's own motion to vacate his conviction.

In the motion, Master wrote, "The CIB has concluded, based on an extensive investigation of Bush's claims that has included interviews of dozens of witnesses, attorneys, and scientists; a reexamination of forensic evidence presented in the case; and an evaluation of the newly discovered alternative suspect's potential involvement in the crime, that Bush's claims [of innocence] are substantiated."

The motion goes on through fifty-five pages of description covering all the points on which Keith's conviction had hinged, systematically shooting them down. It concludes that the conviction was "fatally undermined" by the withholding of exculpatory evidence—known in the legal world as a Brady violation, named after the 1963 Supreme Court case, *Brady v. Maryland*. It requires prosecutors to turn over all evidence that could potentially exonerate a defendant in a criminal case.

Hypothetically, the district attorney's office could have decided that even though the old case was flawed, they wanted to re-prosecute Keith—essentially starting his trial over from scratch. But Master went a step further, saying that the evidence indicates that Keith is "actually innocent of the crimes with which he was convicted."

So it was that on May 22, 2019, Keith, his family and friends, his legal team, and the district attorney's office all came together in Riverhead before Suffolk County Judge Anthony Senft in a unanimous call for the 1976 conviction to be overturned.

Sini, in a rare move for a district attorney, appeared personally before Senft to ask the judge to grant the defense's motion.

Senft obliged. He apologized on behalf of the criminal justice system for what had happened all those years ago, when a different cast of characters serving the same roles had acted to push a seventeen-year-old boy into a lifetime of unnecessary misery.

"Mr. Bush, I cannot give you back that which was taken from you in the 1970s," Senft told Keith. "But I can give you back your presumption of innocence."

Later the same day in a news conference, Sini made it clear that he believes Keith's argument that he was railroaded by a corrupt system.

"Mistakes happen in all aspects of our lives," he said. "But there was intentional misconduct here."

And for the first time since 1975, Keith was truly a free man: no handcuffs, no prison bars, no parole officers.

With his exoneration, Keith became national and international news. His name graced the pages of the *New York Times*, *USA Today* and the *Wall Street Journal*. His story was picked up by *The Independent* and the *Daily Mail* in the U.K. His voice carried over the radio, and his image was plastered on television screens.

And rightfully so. Even a cursory understanding of his struggle and this final victory would be compelling. Thirty-three years in prison is a long time for anyone, much less an innocent man.

But Keith's case is even more extraordinary. It's among the longest periods of time for a homicide exoneration in American history, according to data from the National Registry of Exonerations. In New York state, only one other innocent man lived under his conviction longer: Paul Gatling, who was convicted of murder in 1964 and exonerated in 2016. Unlike Keith, though, Gatling only spent ten years in prison, having had his sentence commuted by former New York Governor Nelson Rockefeller in 1974.

These astonishing data points may be one of the few ways in which Keith gained from his repeated insistence of innocence before the Parole Board. Remember, he could have been released after twenty years, but a teenager's lifetime was tacked on because he refused to play the guilt game.

Not that anyone would ever want this kind of exceptionality.

Perhaps, though, there are larger lessons to be gained from this debacle. The police and courts in Suffolk County—indeed, nationwide—are undergoing a period of soul-searching spurred in part by missteps like those that occurred in Keith's case. The district attorney's office certainly seems to be heading in a better direction by placing more emphasis on the truth and less on short-term victories.

Other criminal justice reforms around the country are taking hold, from the institutionalization of body cameras to the loosening of mandatory minimum sentences and initiatives aimed at better integrating former convicts into society.

You probably don't know this, but Keith had also fought for years for criminal justice reform, with unprecedented results.

Still, anticorruption units and prison reforms are fragile; they're human institutions that only work if the people involved with them believe in them and make efforts to preserve them.

There is also much more that needs to change. There's little doubt that race played a role in Keith's case, and on this front his situation is hardly unusual. The National Registry of Exonerations released a report in 2017 noting that although African Americans only account for thirteen percent of the American population, they represented forty-seven percent of exonerees in the registry as of October 2016. The report estimated that innocent Black people were about seven times more likely to be convicted of murder than innocent White people. And cases involving innocent Black defendants were twenty-two percent more likely to involve police misconduct than those of White defendants.

Minority communities in the U.S. have had a contentious relationship with law enforcement for the entire history of the country. African Americans have a deep distrust of police and courts that continues to this day. It is an understandable distrust fostered by cases like Keith's. It creates victims on all sides.

The advent of cell phone videos of police interactions with African Americans has cast a stark light on some of the racial issues that persist in policing. Few people in Black communities are shocked by them—they've been talking about these problems for decades. Nevertheless, they have forced all Americans to confront this unpleasant reality.

Even these images, though, only reveal a small slice of the broader obstacles minorities face in the criminal justice system. Most cops, lawyers, and judges are not consciously racist. But they inhabit a system built on a heritage of bias and racism. It's embedded in laws, policies, and practices, often unspoken and unrecognized. Even the most upstanding officer or judge can become beholden to it simply by not paying constant attention to how it taints everything. It takes constant vigilance to cut through the effects of this racial legacy.

The certificate of disposition dismissal, the official document from the court confirming Keith's new status, states:

"The abovementioned dismissal is a termination of the criminal action in favor of the accused and pursuant to section 160.60 of the criminal procedure law 'the arrest and prosecution shall be deemed a nullity, and the accused shall be restored, in contemplation of law, to the status occupied before the arrest and prosecution.'"

Though Keith might be "restored" in the eyes of the law, it is of course impossible for him to be truly restored. The courts are not time machines; they cannot give him the last forty-plus years of his life back. They cannot restore his former faith in the justice system or the time he missed with his family and friends. They can't even restore his reputation among the albeit small number of people who will stubbornly cling to the notion that he committed this crime, despite all the evidence to the contrary.

Although the certificate of disposition dismissal also sealed all the official records and papers relating to Keith's case, most of those documents have been circulating for years. His name has been listed under the sex offender registry for a decade. There's no putting that genie back in its bottle.

What's doubly troubling is that Sherese will possibly never have justice either. Jones is dead. Many of the other witnesses to the events of that night have also died. Time has clouded the memories of others. The physical evidence deteriorates further by the day.

On the day of his exoneration, Keith himself chose to call attention to this continued injustice for Sherese.

"Although this is a very special day for me and my family, it is also a sad day for Sherese Watson and her family, because there was never proper closure. Sherese died a violent and senseless death, and it's sad that there were possibilities at that time that would have enabled those authorities to look at this case and objectively seek out the truth—and ultimately bring proper closure for Sherese and for her family. But because they deliberately and intentionally undermined the duties and responsibilities entrusted in them, their family left the courthouse hating me for decades for something that I had literally nothing to do with. And that's an injustice in and of itself."

Keith may be free, but he will never find true justice. Neither will Sherese. Justice would be if he hadn't been charged in the first place. Justice would be if the police and prosecutors had honestly pursued the real leads that they knew existed surrounding this murder. Justice was an option in the 1970s—not today.

The only viable option today is to establish retroactive laws of accountability against offenders like detectives Dennis Rafferty and August Stahl. Two detectives comfortably living on one of the highest paying pensions in the country. A Suffolk County apology to Keith and continued pensions to corrupt detectives is a major contradiction.

Brandon T. Bisceglia

The Birth of a Movement

LATE GRANDFATHERS OF THE NTA MOVEMENT

EDDIE (KABAKA) ELLIS, co-designer, and creator of the Non-Traditional Approach was also a co-founder of the think tank at Green Haven prison. He introduced the NTA to the country and established himself as an expert in criminal justice reform.

Eddie Ellis and Cardell "Blood" Shaird in Woodbourne prison.

CARDELL (BLOOD) SHAIRD, the renowned high priest of the New Yor State prison system was the Malcolm X Black Study teacher. He was an original member of the think tank and NTA contributor. The cultural foundation of the NTA Movement was laid by Blood.

LARRY WHITE was the primary designer of The Non-Traditional Approach and builder of PAC and its annual legislative conference at Green Haven prison.

DR. GARRY MENDEZ, The National Trust, were one of the first community leader to work with the Green Haven Think Tank and sponsor of The Resurrection Study Group.

In the mid-1980s, the late Larry White and Eddie Ellis, two prisoners serving life sentences, engaged in their own studies, research, and analysis concerning the overwhelming incarceration rate of Blacks and Latinos in the New York state prison system. Initially, these findings were presented through organizational forums and class settings at the Green Haven prison in New York state.

These two men set out to build a new prison movement centered around a concept they developed while at Green Haven Prison. Both men were original members of the Green Haven Prison Think Tank, consisting of elderly prisoners with life sentences and decades of years behind bars.

The think tank is where these men began investigating and further developing their analysis of the New York State crime problem. Its core members: Eddie Ellis, Larry White, Cardell Shaird, Charles Gale, and Lawrence Hayes, to name a few, participated in the research and study until the NTA was developed. This think tank Entity operated under a Quakers Exodus Group under the care of their strongest supporter, Senior Chaplain, the Rev. Ed Muller.

During this period, these men began questioning and conversing around the racial disparities in the criminal justice system. Every facility they came from or went to, they both agreed: there was an overwhelming percentage of prisoners who were either Black or Latino, while criminal justice prison officials and employees, in every branch of the criminal justice system, were overwhelming White.

These numbers were so high, the men were left to conclude that something was taking place in these specific communities that was not taking place in the general society.

Curiosity led to discussions, and discussions led to additional disturbing questions that required even more answers. To answer those questions, Larry and Eddie began their search through the pages of history for the time when Blacks and Latinos became the state new majority of prisoners.

These disturbing questions and the historical facts, that provided answers to those questions, are what establish the basis for this intimate relationship between the criminal justice system and the Black/Latino communities. At that time, no one was talking about this relationship in the way that these two prisoners had defined it. This relationship was initially documented as "bridging." The concept began as an outline and later developed into "The Direct Relationship."

The inquisitive minds of Larry and Eddie would ultimately lead to an in-depth study of the criminal justice system and the direct relationship it created with Black/Latino communities. By the latter part of the 1980s, the research conducted by Larry and Eddie had evolved into a profound comprehensive analytical Lense called, "The Non-Traditional Approach to Criminal and Social Justice (NTA)."

Larry and Eddie shared their visions about how best to use the NTA as a teaching tool for prisoners. Like the other elderly prisoners in the Exodus group, they both knew these teachings had to be passed down and would become essential to the awakening process for the proliferated influx of younger prisoners entering the back end of the criminal justice system.

Many of these young prisoners had life sentences and serious ongoing beefs that would only continue in prison settings and yard battlegrounds but would increase the prison environment with violence instead of a collective movement for prison reform and community restoration.

Larry and Eddie designed the NTA as a teaching tool to change negative mindsets and reintroduce a new way of looking at the criminal justice system and the role of the prisoner as participatory players in the perpetuation of the problem.

The NTA makes it clear, as a participant in victimizing one's community, offenders carry with them accountability to the very communities they have negatively affected. This accountability is a commitment to self-recovery in preparation for a return to their community as an asset with a sense of community.

George Prendez was one of the first Latino prisoners mentored by Eddie and Larry in the NTA. George embraced the NTA and would serve as a key player in recruiting Latinos and teaching the Latino perspective of the NTA to Green Haven's Latino prison population.

Like so many others, I would also play a role in the NTA movement as Kishaka (Kichaka). I was introduced to Eddie by Kenneth (Cush) Kirkland days prior to the Green Haven prison lockdown demonstration on September 11th, 1989.

Cush bridged the relationship based on a document written by me calling for a Council of Elders. Cush approached me, excited about a group of old timers he had met in one of the back rooms in the Protestant Center in the J-School area. Cush told me he had found the Council of Elders and that "the brothers are deep." They had obviously brought him into one of their classes and left an impression upon him.

Cush wanted me to meet them. Two days later, I met a man who introduced himself as Eddie Ellis. Ellis was suave and distinguished, his mannerisms were filled with confidence, and his approach was direct. He was also a great teacher and mentor.

Ellis told me he was teaching a youth leadership program. Cush referred me to him. Eddie wanted to know if I was interested. I agreed, at which time the decision was to wait until after the demonstration.

A few days prior to that demonstration, the late Cardell Shaird (aka "Blood"), the Malcolm X Black Studies instructor and member of the Green Haven Think Tank, came to get me. Blood brought me to a secret meeting held between prisoners who argued the pros and cons for or against the lockdown. Most of the younger prisoners wanted to shut down the prison as the domino effect for all the other prisons in the state.

In a heated exchange, one particularly fierce and articulate old-timer strongly opposed the stoppage, offering his own viable alternatives. In essence, he argued that a prison shutdown/work stoppage for demands would only result in massive transferring around the state. He argued in favor of bringing issues to its source. The community and those departments who made the laws.

I had never seen him before, nor did I know who he was. I later found out his name was Larry "Luqman" White, sometimes referred to as "Papa Rage." One of the grandfathers of the New Prison Movement. Luqman, a visionary and great organizer, was also a mentor and great teacher. He was instrumental in also pushing me up in leadership.

As this secret meeting ended, most of the prisoners, all young, took a position that could be summarized as "Fuck these old-timers! On the eleventh, the shit is on."

At that time, I did not know Eddie, Blood, and Larry were all a member of the Green Haven Think Tank and were serving as the fuel, during the 1980s and 1990s, for Green Haven's educational opportunities.

On September 11th, 1989, well over five hundred prisoners refused to leave our cells to participate in a work stoppage. The issues of concern: prisoners' right to vote, good-time, and minimum wages. All to no avail. At least to the general prisoner population, but not to Larry and Eddie.

After the lockdown/work stoppage fell through, resulting in keep-lock time and massive transfers, the co-designers of the NTA and those who remained set out to embark upon a different kind of rehabilitative model, an NTA empowerment model, with innovative lenses that focused on self-empowerment, civic duty, and social justice reform.

In 1988, Eddie and George went to Sing-Sing prison to participate in a one-year master's degree program in theology from the Theological Seminary. In 1989, upon their return to Green Haven prison, Eddie and George drafted a pilot project. The proposal was submitted to the Rev. Dr. Ernest Davis Jr., Senior Chaplain in the Protection center.

The proposal was approved as a pilot project and was called Faith & Life: Religious Education Project: Inter Faith Action Group. Eddie and George used praxis to establish three NTA programs, with the third being taught by Larry White.

These three programs would become the first leadership programs created by Larry and Eddie, with George teaching its Latino component. The primary objective of these three Faith & Life groups were to reach young prisoners and teach them the NTA.

Larry was not a graduate of the Theological Seminar. With the backing of Rev. Muller and presentations by Eddie, Larry, and George, Green Haven senior prison chapel, the late Rev. Dr. Ernest Davis Jr., provided a third classroom and office space in the protestant center for the educational initiation of the NTA. The Faith & Life: Religious Education Project: Inter Faith Groups would eventually change their names to:

- Resurrection Study Group (RSG)
- Liberation Study Group (LSG)
- Conciencia Study Group (CSG)

The office was immediately transformed from a basic clerical setting into an intellectual outpost for tactical and strategic brainstorming. Those of us heavily engaged in this task used the clerk office for what would be renamed, "The War Room." Carl Dukes (RSG core member) was the second clerk for the three Faith & Life programs.

He was also recorder keeper of important data developed in the war room. As clerk, he was privileged to just about all the ideas that went into the growth process of the NTA. Carl knew firsthand the key contributors to the development of the NTA and the sometime heated disputes that took place between its co-founders and other emerging leaders in the evolution of the NTA movement, including Carl himself.

The war room would become the place where rationality, planning, strategizing, and executing led to major developments. All and all, the war room was the place that seeded the birth of a movement and the intellectual battleground from its co-creators, leaders, developers, and contributors.

After the prison demonstration, all those placed under keep-lock status instead of a disciplinary transfer became the selection pool from which to build a movement. By Green Haven becoming one of the prison education centers of the state, more than enough was left behind to fill the Faith & Life programs.

The first task was to implement the Faith & Life study groups. These groups would become the first three groups specifically geared toward creating a new breed of leaders that would become the practitioners and defenders of the NTA analysis.

The second task was to build a prisoner movement coalition, unifying prisoner groups and organizations under the umbrella of an NTA approach. To initiate and build a prison movement, Larry and Eddie went around the prison presenting the NTA while soliciting membership into what would be called the "Political Action Committee, (PAC)."

The PAC consisted of a coalition of socially conscious prisoner organizations/groups at Green Haven. PAC evolved out of the NTA analysis and was the testing ground for the New Prison Movement.

The PAC's mission was to establish, support, and encourage connections between prisoners and their communities; to assist in the development of community-based program models; and to serve as a catalyst for change. The PAC motto was: "It is time that state prisoners participate in solving the critical problems that affect their own community."

The PAC initiated and cosponsored annual legislative conferences at Green Haven. These conferences involved PAC representatives, community leaders, and legislators from those communities most affected by crime and the state prison system.

The NTA called for community involvement in prison programming and policy determination. This was particularly imperative in New York state, where the criminal justice system was infested with institutional racism eating delectably off irresponsible criminal behavior intensified in socially derived targeted communities. The NTA called for socially conscious prisoners to defend this position and help solve this problem.

The first test came at the beginning. Just as George Prendez began to teach the Latino component of the NTA, he was transferred to another facility. The members of Conciencia never missed a beat. Many of these men became mentors to other prisoners and took on greater roles in fulfilling the NTA community civic duty commitment.

Walter "Horses" Figueroa, transitioned into Conciencia leadership and became its instructor for the Latino prison population after George Prendez transferred from Green Haven prison. The co-founders assisted with the NTA, while Horses and Conciencia created their own Latino curriculum and taught the NTA from a Latino perspective.

These co-founders also made it clear about their intentions on contacting community leaders and legislators from the Black/Latino community to present the NTA findings and the issues raised around the work stoppage/prison demonstration.

The first and most important community leader to embrace the NTA analysis was Dr. Alice Green out of the New York Civil Liberties Union in Albany, N.Y., and as Executive Director of the Center for Law & Justice. Dr. Green understands the NTA just as well as the prisoners learning it in the classroom. As poof of her commitment, she made the biggest push that made it possible for the Annual Legislative Conference to convene.

The PAC held its first legislative conference in February 1990. In addition to socially and politically conscious prisoners, also in attendance were members of the Black & Puerto Rican Legislative Caucus, Dr. Green, and prison officials.

The purpose of the conference was to provide prisoners with the opportunity to address community leaders and legislators about the impact of the NYS prison system on Black/Latino communities. To seize the opportunity for state prisoners to develop and maintain contact with their community and legislators' representatives to assist the community in solving this problem. Thus, the annual legislative conference was initiated.

January, the following year, 1991, Eddie was transferred to Woodbourne prison. In addressing the RSG class, Eddie placed the leadership and responsibility of RSG in my hands.

In February, I gave a presentation on the RSG program at the Second Annual Legislative Conference sponsored by PAC. The primary purposes of this conference were to further lay out the NTA analysis, discuss the issue of Earned Incentive Allowance, and to present community specific programs developed by prisoners.

The Political Action Committee would be renamed: "Prisoner's Alliance with Community (PAC)" with a new highlighted theme later added to the front page of the NTA's 1997 revision: "It is time that state prisoners participate in solving the critical problems that affect their own community."

The following year, Richard "Black-God" Jackson (RSG core member) gave a presentation at the third annual conference. The conference lacked central office policy makers and community organizations from the NYC area. Six legislative representatives were present. The conference raised the need for a "Criminal Justice Subcommittee" and "Community Specific Oversight Board."

At the fourth annual conference held in February 1993, the intent was to bring together the four social categories of participants in the relationship between all parties involved and to commit each party to membership of the conference. To reach agreements on protocols, procedures, and objectives to guide the conference effectively toward resolution to problem solving.

Following the end of the fourth annual legislative conference, the NTA movement would encounter internal conflicts initiated by outside agitators and prison officials. But the expansion project enabled it to spread throughout the state prison system and in the communities as well.

Many of the members of the Green Haven think tank were great visionaries, historians, organizers, teachers, and initiators with reputations for producing results.

This original wave of leadership earned and deserved their titles of "Grandfathers of the New Prison Movement." These men knew exactly want they wanted and the determination to achieve it can only be defined as relentless, and relentless they were!

This movement may not have been possible without the initial community assistance and involvement from Dr. Garry Mendez, The National Trust for the Development of African American Men; Rev. Ed Muller, Senior Chaple at Green Haven; Dr. Alice Green, Center for Law & Justice; and the late Raymond Broaddus, Ass. Deputy Commissioner for NYS Corrections.

This first wave of leadership would establish the foundation for new leadership. Out of that leadership, I would emerge.

Resurrection: The Empowerment Model

THE RESURRECTION STUDY GROUP

The late EDDIE ELLIS was a renowned community leader and a member of the Black Panther Party in the 1960s and 1970s. His connections with the Black Liberation Army and the Revolutionary Action Movement led to his targeting by J. Edgar Hoover's counterintelligence program. Wrongly accused, Eddie served over 23 years in prison.

During his incarceration, he earned a master's degree from the New York Theological Seminary. He co-founder the Green Haven Think Tank and the Non-Traditional Approach to Criminal & Social Justice (NTA). After his release, Eddie introduced the NTA as the "Seven Neighborhood Study," a pioneering analytical approach to criminal justice reform, to the nation, thereby establishing himself as an expert in the field.

His achievements go far beyond, and his dedication to change is reflected in the enduring integrity of his legacy. Eddie was a true pioneer and a colossus among his peers. His life contribution is a celebration for all those he has touched and a revelation for all those on the path to recovery.

Keith ([Kishaka] Bush was appointed head of the Resurrection Study Group by Eddie Ellis in 1991, when Eddie was transferred to another facility. Keith served over 33 years in prison and 12 years on parole for a crime he did not commit. In a shocking turn of events in New York State, Keith was exonerated after more than 44 years of legal battles.

While incarcerated, Keith became an organizer, program developer, and facilitator. He advanced the Resurrection Study Group and played a pivotal role in establishing a strong community-prisoner linkage with The National Trust for the Development of African American Men. Under Keith's leadership, the Resurrection program expanded throughout the state prison system, becoming one of the most productive prison programs in the nation.

Keith is also an authority on the Non-Traditional Approach and a key contributor to the Prisoner Alliance with Community (consisting of joint prisoner organizations and groups). He has established himself as an initiator, an innovator, and a champion for criminal justice reform in his own right. He is currently engaged in several innovative projects.

By: Stanley (Jamel) Bellamy
Resurrection Director

In the month of October 1989, Eddie Ellis initiated the Faith & Life youth leadership NTA program. Within the first year of the program, its official name would be officially changed to: "The Resurrection Study Group (RSG)."

RSG would become the place where I would develop a better understanding of the criminal justice system and hold a leadership role in the New Prison Movement.

Teaching the NTA in a classroom setting is not the same as reading the document itself. Each week, Eddie stood before the class and was authoritative in his delivery. His Afrocentric views and understanding of the criminal justice system placed him on a collision course with opposing experts in the same field.

We were constantly being reminded of the importance of understanding the NTA analysis because it would be our responsibility to provide solutions or viable alternatives to the problems of crime and prison.

Eddie regularly reminded us of our responsibility to "defend the analysis." As he put it, "Many people will try to prove you wrong, including the so-called experts."

Eddie prepared RSG by giving the members the necessary teaching experience needed to instruct classes on the NTA.

We were required to give presentations, write articles, and look through newspapers and magazines for possible community linkages and resources. If RSG were to play its part in creating cadres of leaders to return to their communities to help address the problem of crime and social justice, it was necessary to align ourselves with the communities.

Eddie's teaching of the NTA had most of us looking forward to class while enthusiastically functioning in high gear.

The components of the RSG curriculum were discussed, structured, developed, and typed by Eddie, Tyrone Hill, Cush, and me. RSG set up its first expansion program, sending out members on their first mission. An RSG creed was used to recite before and at the end of each class or joint gathering.

Seminars with religious and community leaderships, i.e., Rev. Dr. Lillian Brown on behalf of the late Rev. Dr. Calvin Butts and Dr. Garry Mendez, were conducted to discuss and seek linkage with outside supporters. RSG participated in discussion forums and gave presentations to other groups around the facility. Our special events offered to the prison population drew a lot of interest from younger prisoners to join.

The late Theodore Baker, former President of Peregrine Jay Cee, a prison chapter, provided space to RSG to teach the NTA under their Individual Leadership Program. In a bold decision, Theordore changed the organization from Peregrine Jay Cee to Association for Community Teamwork (ACT).

I was one of the members who worked closely with Eddie in the initial stages of RSG. Eddie brought me in as the second representative for RSG to the PAC and began pushing me into a leadership position.

In 1991, Eddie was notified of a transfer to Woodbourne prison. Concerned about the foundation Eddie had built the NTA upon, he was also concerned about its growth and opposition. Eddie felt that I was the best choice to lead RSG on its mission. In the presence of Larry, I confidently assured Eddie that the work would be done.

But after Eddie's departure, external forces attempted to initiate internal conflict within the group. A few members quit, assuming after Eddie left RGS would no longer have anything to offer. A few other members left after being told Pan-Africanism contradicted their religious faith. Members suddenly rejected the term Africa, sparking a minor linguistic classroom debate.

Jealousy and dissatisfaction by a few members arose regarding me being in leadership and the future of RSG. My conviction would also become a subject matter.

A few of these attacks were also directed at Eddie, Larry, and me. Outsiders tried to poison the NTA with lies that the three of us were using the men to get out of prison. It even carried over to the PAC. None of these lies perpetuated by jealous outsiders of the PAC would stand. The infrastructure and outside bridge were too strong to brake.

In RSG, I restructured the program and sought to diffuse any possible cover plots and internal turmoil. I also restructured RSG into three components: basic, advanced, and the core members.

The basic class offered the general population an education out of the RSG curriculum. The advanced component dealt with the curriculum's transitional phase, application, and other intermitted instructions. These men were required to set up projects for proactive task-oriented missions.

The core members would become the collective decision-making body that must take on the responsibility as Directors of the various projects, teachers of the curriculum, and served as representatives to the PAC. I identified the main problem and confronted it head on.

Michael "Lord Amsu" Grey was appointed as head of RSG security, and RSG wrote it's "code of conduct."

RSG was placed back on track, and new members were brought into the group.

RSG held a fellowship seminar with Jean Dumber, Dr. Mary Wilder and Mr. Carmille Smith based on linkage or sponsorship. Mr. Carmille Smith was committed to RSG sponsorship.

For changing its name to ACT, the prison administration threatened to dissolve the ACT organization without sponsorship. President Theodore made a request to me for usage of Mr. Carmille Smith as a sponsor until one could be found. To save ACT, I agreed. That decision led to dissatisfaction among some members in the group.

ACT went on to become a strong supporter of prisoner leadership and empowerment efforts in the interest of the Black/Latino community.

The late Dr. Garry Mendez would eventually become an essential player in fulfilling the community involvement section of the NTA.

Garry worked closely with socially conscious prisoners in the early 1980s, he also held the position of Director of the Administration of Justice for the National Urban League. He established The National Trust in response to the multitude of problems faced by men in African American communities.

Garry had been involved in the early development of the NTA and had also developed several other initiatives, including one called "Crime is Not a Part of Our Black Heritage." In December 1990, RSG invited him to Green Haven to conduct a leadership workshop for RSG.

RSG continued to look to Garry as a possible sponsor. Garry and I engaged in ongoing dialogue until Garry agreed to seek funding for a prison pilot leadership program.

The central theme of this community/prisoner relationship was to further train and develop a cadre of leaders inside the prison system and prepare them to return to their communities to provide new leadership upon release. Garry provided professional, technical, and any other training the men would need.

With the RSG/TNT relationship, we committed ourselves to creating and facilitating community commitment programs. We established the first computer lab in a maximum-security facility. We offered computer literacy to the general prison population in the mid-1990s.

This was during the time I began typing the earlier sections of my handwritten autobiography. In prison, I went to school for computers and helped create a computer lab. Its amazing how I would be sent back to prison for using a computer (no internet access) for finishing this same story.

We conducted seminars, workshops, and designed programs the administration denied but later coopted. We began successfully spreading our training throughout the state prison system and a few prisons in other states. Some of our deported core members have taught while some continue to teach the RSG/TNT training in some of the Caribbean countries.

Many of these members went back to school and acquired associate's, bachelor's, or master's degrees. Three members have achieved their doctoral degree and like so many of the others, they have returned to their communities to help rebuild them.

The most intriguing part of this history is that just about all the RSG/TNT core members were doing life sentences. Most of us had no idea if we would ever get out of prison.

The commitment we made did not offer us any promise of release as an incentive. Yet we consistently stayed on this path, educating thousands of prisoners since the 1980s and community youth as a civic duty commitment.

We've had positive impacts on our families and extended our civic duties to the communities. As of 2016, many of these men have earned their release and occupy leadership roles in their own communities.

Some have become authors, teachers, or entrepreneurs. They've helped create programs and organizations. They are contributing to the empowerment of their communities.

Although I was one of the leaders and contributor to this great endeavor, the restrictive and stringent parole supervision imposed upon me didn't allow me to offer services to my community. Instead, I served as an adviser and continued my services behind the scenes.

Those left behind in prisons are still fulfilling their commitment to the RSG/TNT creed. Their sentences have stretched on for over thirty years because of constant parole denials. Nonetheless, their disappointments have had no impact on their newfound obligations.

The level of personal growth, output of productivity, and degree of impact these men have made within themselves and upon their loved-ones and communities makes the NTA an approach worthy of attention.

Green Haven is where I made my greatest transformational strides. I developed myself and made contributions to others along the way. I like to think I represented myself with integrity and chose a movement to deter crime/recidivism and fight for criminal justice reform for the betterment of the community.

I went from student to RSG Director, Project Build President, PAC representative/chairman, inside coordinator for RSG/NTA, facilitator, co-director, and program developer.

I helped to write sections of the agendas for the PAC conferences. I wrote several position papers and the secondary structure for the PAC annual conference, the Oversight Board. I helped to establish community linkage in what would become one of the most successful sponsored community/prisoner relationships in the country.

I worked with prisoners and community organizations to help raise money in two fundraising drives to help children. I was honored by ACT with a prestigious individual award in recognition for outstanding community service.

For me the NTA took on greater significance, aside from the statistics, data, and other empirical knowledge. The NTA analysis served as a bridge between my abuse by the criminal justice system and the abuse inflicted upon of my African American ethnicity since the signing of the Emancipation Proclamation. Apparently, I had personal reasons for joining.

There were a lot of valuable lessons I learned in the process. Making a collective contribution is far more difficult than I had anticipated. It was a stressful and demanding endeavor, but worth the investment.

But I wore deeply engrained scars associated with the nature of my conviction. I still had that stigma that had always followed me. Some tried to use it to mask their jealousy, envy, and dissent. Some even tried to secretly discredit my leadership by attempting to assassinate my character.

As one of many participants in this movement, one thing is certain, the fruit of my labor stood on its own merits, and my determination to rise above defamation remained intact. I had grown into an intellectual in my own right and handled myself with ease against these assaults.

The external and internal conflict associated with this movement were minor irritants. During those brief periods of turmoil, I followed through with the promises I made to Eddie and Larry. That promise was to help advance the mission by keeping the course in the direction dictated by the NTA. I did my part and did it well.

But I did not do it alone. The RSG/TNT had become more than a leadership program. Its core members had seized over seventy percent of the leadership in the general prison population and at one time almost ninety percent of the PAC representation that led to some complaints that RSG had monopolize the PAC and its decision making.

In RSG/TNT, I learned a lot from and exchanged with some highly intelligent men who took responsibility for their actions in a way never seen before. If I had to enter any intellectual arena to battle, I'd choose to battle with RSG/TNT."

In 1997, my classification status was suddenly changed from maximum to minimum security. This sudden change in status removed me from the center stage of the NTA movement into the upstate wilderness of the state prison system to further punish me for continuing to maintain my innocence.

My transfer from Green Haven to Fishkill prison became another battleground of attack against me for my stance of innocence. This battle would again take place in the federal court system. At this stage in my development, I was more than ready. I immediately went after Corrections for violating my constitutional right for believing in the Bible and for upholding and honoring God's name.

The Empowerment Journey

On this journey I constructed my own lifestyle that I considered as my best option for victory!

A prisoner doing a life sentence for a crime he often complained he didn't commit became overwhelmed by the pressure of his predicament. In his difficulties dealing with his false imprisonment and the ugly reality of prison life, he made some poor decisions. He would have been a good candidate to test the RSG model.

He was a close friend with one of RSG's core members, who was trying to help him straighten out his life. With a sentence of thirty-three years to life in prison, he just couldn't see himself completing the journey and oftentimes confessed that he would rather die in a way bordering on suicide than to do thirty-three years. Locking on the East Side of the prison, he was out of control.

One of the members brought him into the class. After a few classes he showed some signs of progress and then disappeared. The negative influences kept pulling him away. He would promise to try to stay out of trouble and ask that we not give up on him.

We were helping him prior to him being sent back to Rikers Island for a court hearing on his case. But when he returned, he was just as confused and misguided as he had been prior to his involvement with RSG, especially about the fear of doing thirty-three years. All he kept talking about was that he couldn't do that much time, he was going to die in prison.

When someone told him how much time I had done so far in prison and was also innocent, he went mentally crazy and vowed he would rather die than to do that much time, and he meant it. When he would ask me for advice, I would tell him he was trapped in a pendulum. It was throwing him all over the place.

He needed to find his own "seat of power" and take control so he could prepare himself to fight. I didn't have any advice for someone who would rather die without putting up a fight. I told him to pull away from the things in the yard that kept him in trouble. Learn how to get back in touch with himself while RSG helped him to develop a road map. He would agree and disappear again into the madness he thought could mask his reality.

He got so involved in the deleterious aspects of prison life that he stopped attending RGS classes and affiliating with the membership. Shortly thereafter, he was murdered in Green Haven's prison yard.

Choosing that harmful path over RGS may have contributed to his own victimization. Unfortunately, the life he chose fulfilled his own prophecy in a sad, sad way.

Sometimes it's hard to see if one is consciously embracing a life of destruction or is searching for light amid darkness. Wishing for death over a life of terrible suffering can sometimes lead one astray.

The prisoner murdered in that yard got his wish in the worst way. What's even sadder is that too many young men die this way. Too many of us give up on them too soon.

For me, it's exceedingly painful to see another human being doing a life sentence in prison for a crime they did not commit. Most have no idea of the tribulations they will encounter.

Some may not make it through; they can be doomed by their inability to cope with the excruciating circumstances, the mental and physical demands thrust on them.

Those who do succeed construct survival tools for themselves. As part of the transformation of my own consciousness, I felt it was my responsibility to impart whatever wisdom I'd accumulated to the young prisoners about to embark on such a difficult venture.

Because of the unnecessary death of this young man, I developed a "journey map" to help prisoners "construct a new life." I knew some would take heed, though many would not.

I also knew some of this information would take root slowly, like planted seeds. Though change might not be evident at the conscious level, it could lay dormant within the subconscious until a unique experience caused wisdom to push above the soil. Comprehension does not reach us all at the same time. Many ideas take time to grow. This young man's death is one of the reasons why there is a need for transformative type self-empowerment models.

Engulfed in the same type of captivity, suffering and struggle, I also started my journey lost. But in time, I would develop my own self-growth approach as a reward for an investment I made in developing myself at the physical, mental, and spiritual level.

I created my own self-empowerment approach and built my model on the foundation of an imagery intense internal transformation process. It helped me to unshackle the mental chains that gave me my image of myself instead of me creating myself out of my own image.

I do not have the academic credentials of the so-called experts you may think are best suited to address this issue. Experts do not always know. Imagine if I believed what the so-called experts said about me, I would have died in a prison cage.

At sentencing, the pre-sentence probation officer relied heavily upon the psychological report of school records in their recommendation for extensive incarceration.

According to these records, I was defined as, "emotionally unstable, evasive... Impression is one of a haphazard, goal-less wanderer. The future holds nothing for him, each day is as emotionally deprived as the next... His full-scale I.Q. was placed at 77, intelligence well-below normal." My so-called intelligence was placed just above the borderline of mild mental retardation.

With an I.Q. this low, how did I make it to the 11th grade with one year left to graduate? If there is any validity to these assertions made, then obviously I was being written off by the educational system.

Without the basic education required for self-preservation, the mental capacity to development coupled with the lack of viable marketable skills, according to these experts, I lacked the basic sound judgment and power of decision making.

The probation officer went even further in stating, "This psychological information coupled with crime would indicate the court is faced with a very unstable youth, who requires 'substantial psychiatric therapy' in a structured setting."

How then was I able to develop myself and overcome negative forces that tried to seize the little sanity even the experts denied to me? I could not possibly have developed the insight to free myself let alone survive over four decades in a cage with all the odds stacked against me.

I obviously did not perceive myself that way and in time I would render all assessments made of me void by proving the experts wrong.

Every journey in life is specific and is defined by its own purpose. For me, the purpose of my empowerment was not an option. Being confined to a cage possibly for the rest of my life made it a prerequisite. On this difficult road, I had to prepare myself for what was required of me and the challenges ahead.

Preparation for me meant obtaining better ways to develop myself and how best to maximize the effort needed to reach my goal.

A deep, cleansing, internal and external healing had to first occur before a transformation could take place. Mental toughness, independent thinking, being aggressive and proactive were all important applications to the foundational building blocks of the empowerment process.

Examining and re-examining past experiences, events, and the impact they were having on my life validated this need. It forced me to face my fears, inadequacies, and the need to wage war on ignorance, confusion, and other negative forces that constantly fought for the right to dictate and gain dominance over the enforcer of the self, my willpower.

I turned my attention inward, using my mind as a portal, to search and sense for the inner core of my being where spirit and willpower reside. I adapted techniques discovered from study and personal insight to blend my shattered ego and inner self back into oneness.

I also equipped myself with the necessities needed to protect and shield against the most precious part of the mental region most vulnerable to powerful negative social influences. Never again would I become a victim of dictation and social indoctrination.

The mental blockage that prevented the full flow of consciousness left me victimized by a system far beyond my control. Cursed by injustice, vulnerability reigned supreme over my world. In the beginning, my ignorance had the loudest voice. Whenever it spoke, I listened. Unbeknownst to me, ignorance had never aided anyone, so why would ignorance become an aid to me?

As an adult, making an investment in my growth process

would pay off when a new, transformative lens emerged as the driving force that molded me into becoming an independent thinker, initiator, and fact finder of the truth.

Why must we journey? Because everything in existence is moving even when it appears to be standing still. A journey cannot be possible without movement, as it is without time. Movement gives motion to matter and acts as a vehicle through life. The very nature of human consciousness is to experience itself as the only means for knowing itself.

Experience is self-evident of knowing and existing is the only way to validate it as fact. Life introduces us to who we are. But empowering ourselves, as we journey through life, determines what we become.

My empowerment journey became a self-conscious endeavor. I had to prepare myself for new challenges and the unknown. I needed to discover my potential and maximize my capacity. A deep cleansing/healing and internal/external transformation had to occur before the reconstruction process could begin. Mental toughness and awareness would become the foundational building blocks for this endeavor.

Only in time would I learn that self-empowerment cannot occur without a deep internal transformation. Examining and reexamining past experiences, events, and the impact they were having on my life validated this fact. It forced me to face my fears and inadequacies. It laid bare the need to wage war on my ignorance, confusion, and other destructive forces that had gained dominance over me.

My studies taught me that I had to turn my attention inward, using my mind as a portal through which to search and reflect. I equipped myself with the necessities needed to protect and shield against that part of the mental region most vulnerable to harmful social influences.

Realizing the need to empower myself was due to my victimization as opposed to some kind of remorse or reconciliation for a self-inflicted wrong or act against another.

The moral of my journey is that everyone must empower themselves. By doing so, they will establish a personal connection with their own source of being. This is the place where self-mastery and control can be found. It is also the place where self-awareness and the power of vision reside.

I was also inspired by others along the way. I spent many years walking the prison yard, engaging in intellectual exchange, teaching, and learning from others. Many of these travelers were products of recidivism; some had started their journey before me. But all were trapped in the same depressing place and time.

I placed realization first. I considered coming to terms as the first step process. Realization provided me with a better understanding of my problem areas and brought into focus my liabilities and assets.

It was important for me to be honest with myself. In doing so, I was able to get in touch with my faults and inadequacies. The realization process also became a viable part of identifying my resources (individual capacities, skills, talents, and abilities) as well as external resources (family and community, support agencies, groups, etc.).

Cleansing would be equally important. It was the basis for

healing in the transformation process. Cleansing enabled me to identify, categorize, and break down my weaknesses so they could be addressed accordingly. Cleansing always provides a sense of spiritual renewal and a disdain for negative activities/associations and bad social influences.

The plucking aspect of cleansing is also highly imaginary. I used imagination to dig and uproot negative habits and uncontrolled drives disturbing my balance and distorting my mission. Socially, the plucking process simply involved a disassociation with dangerous human influences and other forces designed to stagnate growth.

Imagination is vital to the plucking and healing process. With hard work, application, and steadfast commitment, I achieved great rewards of renewal and revitalization. My imagination became the womb to nurture the person I wanted to become. It is the place where vision is born, and creativity resides.

The purging process is worthless if it is not followed by action. I allocated adequate time to self-examination. Most of the time, I chose the late-night hours. They were convenient and quiet, where I would meditate to elicit calmness and emptiness.

After meditation, I would do an overview of my daily activities to examine my performance. I never realized how much I could learn about myself through simple exercises. I wrote down a lot of these observations for reconstruction of the self.

Creating My Own Reality

In a practical sense, knowledge is required for good spiritual, mental, and physical health, as well as a keen sense of focus. In the prison world, my sanity depended upon it. I could not have survived without it. During the many years of my incarceration, I suffered more when I lacked it and benefited most when I gained it.

In the early years of my imprisonment, I continued with my reading, writing, and communication skills but only intermittently. I read some philosophy but tended more toward books about positive thinking and personal development.

I developed the habit in the county jail of taking notes. I wrote down the things I considered important. I put them in the form of lessons or recitations and periodically studied or reviewed them for deeper understanding and internal cleansing. Doing this for years gave me discipline. It also helped me to develop good writing and study habits.

Walking the prison yards and communicating was also an enlightening adventure. It became my only form of travel. Sometimes I would walk the yards for hours with other prisoners, discussing many current and past events on different topics. This form of mental exercise was just another way of stimulating the intellect and creating an outlet. It was a critical part of my development.

Despite the adverse impact my prison experience had on me, it was not the sum of my reality. I was also able to draw from my inner strength and the confidence, hope, and courage it gave me. I also drew from the strength of my immediate family and those who love and supported me.

I lived with the belief that someday I would be free. Even when my days were dim, when my future seemed uncertain, my inner strength would always guide me back to a state of inner peace. This capacity would in time slay the demons that wanted my soul.

Knowledge not only enhanced my personal growth; it also changed my thinking. I was no longer perceiving things linearly. My views had broadened. My thinking extended in multiple directions simultaneously, like the World Wide Web.

I can now see reality more clearly. But this reality has parallel versions of itself. These versions evolve from the infinite pool of probabilities and possibilities. In my mind, an individual experience or event was drawn from a pool of similar probable versions. I needed to be more involved in drawing from this field to increase my chances of bringing into being a reality more favorable to me.

This kind of thinking, difficult to understand until studied, helped me to reevaluate my life. I learned how to effectuate change by utilizing it through the power of my will, and thinking outside the box took on a new meaning.

At my initial parole board appearance, it was made clear to me that Parole had no intention of ever releasing me from prison under my terms. A claim of innocence was totally unacceptable. Even other prisoners thought it was naive to think that way. I would lose another twelve additional years of my life for maintaining that stance.

In the mental world, a self who can control their imagery has access to all sorts of power. Even the kind that heals the spirit, mind, and body. Prayer is the offering of a gift(s). Good deeds are the rewards at the fountain where revitalization and divine consumption takes place.

I no longer saw myself as someone spending the rest of my life in prison. I could perceive that version of myself competing with other versions for the right to emerge as the conscious choice who would bring me home. It felt like I had finally made it to the crossroads. It was at this place, a sort of psychological bridge, where the boy I was and the man I became changed places.

Taking the journey and fulfilling the task was how I mentally freed myself. How I grew into an independent thinker, and how I developed my own approach by using a powerful empowerment tool. It served to diversify my views and increase my awareness.

Becoming an independent thinker helped me to realize and better utilize my strengths, come to terms with my weaknesses and the need to work around them.

It was difficult to break out from the cocoon of this mentally enslaved state and to strive for independence. I needed to take this journey to develop my own transformative and event changing experience. Diversifying my views helped to broaden my awareness. The time and effort invested was worth the commitment.

Mapping Out the Process

In mapping out a problem, the issue must be clearly defined and weighed against the foreseeable odds of succeeding or failing. There is no preparation for the unforeseen. Acknowledge the possibility but don't succumb; direct your will to determination. Determination is like a spiritual rod. If used righteously, it will deliver.

There are variable approaches to self-empowerment. People who take this journey may do so individually or collectively. Some may use other approaches or methods to reach their goals. Every self-empowerment method should have an internal and external component. The internal component is designed to liberate one to be able to practice new spiritual and personal views by using transformative tools for growth. The external component involves a commitment to changing your earthly life into prosperity.

Empowered individuals exhibit high self-esteem, confidence, and a value system that radiates from the core. They display qualities of strength and positive thinking. These individuals strive for value fulfillment beyond the mere desire of wanting without doing. To reach this realm, one must find an inner peace and outer expression of that natural goodness inherent in righteous human judgment.

The road to self-empowerment leads us to an understanding that we are far from powerless. Empowerment removes mental blockages of self-denial and poor self-imagery. It shows us where to find our own strengths. It also allows us to see our own weaknesses and the need to address them.

I never took seriously the importance of self-empowerment until I spent time in solitary confinement. It was there that I began to realize that, unlike those prisoners who sought empowerment through remorse or reconciliation for a crime, I needed a different way to deal with the difficulties of possibly dying in prison.

I could no longer place total trust in the minor successes of merely gaining control over my emotions. This form of progress did represent an aspect of growth, but what I needed was something more complete.

My involvement in programmed activities put me on the right path. I was acquiring knowledge and developing survival skills. I was involved in things I enjoyed doing and was helping other people by passing on useful information (each one teaches one).

But in my own quiet moments, I still couldn't find that internal peace rewarded to those who travel the path to righteousness. I needed an internal "transformation," one powerful enough to guide me through those difficult times.

The prison experience shattered my reality and redefined my view of the world. At times, loneliness, hurt, and anger became my greatest enemies. They fought against my sanity and for possession of my wounded spirit. Living the life of a slave in a prison cage clouded my sensitivity and gave birth to hatred and revenge.

Looking back, it was nothing more than a reminder of how the best years of my life had been washed away in the rainstorm of injustice. I know this was the result of internalizing so much pain. Consequently, that negativity now reigned supreme in my subconscious. It came to me in the form of stress and loneliness. It was a clear warning that this experience was slowly destroying me from the inside.

These signs indicated to me it was time to develop an approach that involved some form of internal transformation. The more I learned, the more apparent it became.

But to do so, I would have to take an internal pilgrimage. The guidance of my ancestors, the blessings of my elders, the wisdom of my family and friends could not take me there. The journey became mine and mine alone.

To travel the road, I would need to develop some fundamental survival skills, to attract the type of people and opportunities that would assist me in my endeavors. I didn't have the luxury of choosing my environment, so I would have to rise above any prison conditions that could interfere with these objectives.

I mapped out my objectives through stages. These self-empowerment stages I defined as: the purging process, spiritual enhancement, personal development, and social commitment. In addition to the empowerment stages, I outlined a comprehensive goal sheet. I chose this approach as my road map to guide me along the way. From this process, I acquired a renewed determination to seize opportunity and achieve goals.

In mapping out the journey, I had to clearly define and properly prepare for both the obvious and the unforeseen in life. I wanted to turn a blind journey into a conscious endeavor. I needed to know the best route to travel.

To construct a new life required the composer of worksheet assignments and study guides. I also conducted prioritization techniques through asset mapping and goal-setting strategies.

After formulating a self-empowerment guide, I wanted to find out what rewards it would offer me.

Purging was the first stage. Self-examination, realization, coming to terms, and cleansing (mental plucking/healing) are all essential purging ingredients and foundational to the transformation process. Before engaging in a purging and cleansing process, realization would be my way of coming to terms with myself. The purging process allowed me to begin uprooting negative thinking and bad habits, cleansing, and fertilizing new soil for the birth of a new reality. But this new reality lacked substance.

Spiritual Enhancement was my second but most important stage. There was a time during my incarceration when my faith in God had been shattered. Prayer and worship were replaced with loneliness, suffering, and confusion. The urgency of struggle and survival dictated my approach. I wasn't connected to a core. I couldn't interpret divine guidance if it was sent to me.

Personal Development became the third stage. I started off by seeking a basic understanding of who I am and what it is I am striving to become. Self-development involves a commitment to excellence. To reach that goal, I needed to bring more meaning into my life. I also needed to determine my skills or lack thereof and prepare for the challenges ahead.

I started by exploring my past. Writing my story enabled me to unearth major events in my life, which shaped my perception. Discovery of who I am also involved learning more about my family tree and the characteristics that define me racially and culturally. I selected family and cultural principles that could enhance my personal development. I use my African/Native

American historical framework as the lens through which I view my world culturally as a person and humanitarian.

Outlining a personal development chart is like creating a plan. It involves developing approaches, identifying, and galvanizing the appropriate resources. It also includes knowing the logistics and implementation process. On my goal sheet there is a personal development chart that has a "personal contract" section that describes important personal commitments. Good health, freedom, and proper hygiene are prime examples.

Through my leadership training from The National Trust for the Development of African American Men, I acquired some excellent skills in interpersonal communication, access mapping, conceptual and analytical thinking, computer literacy, and journal writing. I put together a tracking system for my goals so I could determine if progress was being made and continued to rely upon self-study and research.

Social Commitment was the fourth and final stage of my self-empowerment. This is the expansion commitment: self, family/friends, ethnic, community, world. This is my way of reaching out to others. It would be selfish of me to travel through life benefiting from others without trying to return the blessing or leave something beneficial behind.

To be effective in exercising a social commitment would require me to decide what I was willing to commit to. As an African American ethnic-centric identity group, my social commitment starts there.

My commitment and concerns also belong to the fate of our species and the planet kinds enough to host us. Social commitment includes valuing life, being concerned for others, and a desire to help change negative conditions.

I developed a goal sheet to prioritize and better scrutinize my developments. To bring about the best possible results, I needed to follow through with a course of action. The theoretical framework for self-empowerment was not enough. The primary objective was to use my time wisely so that upon release I would return as mentally prepared and physically healthy as possible.

I designed my goal sheet in accordance with the four stages of self-empowerment. For example, my sheet started with a priority list of the most important goals in my life. I followed the same pattern by setting goals in stages. To achieve these goals, I outlined an "action plan" of at least five specific things I needed to do to reach my goals.

In another section of my goal sheet, I identified bad habits and poor qualities. In a third section, I recorded my skills, abilities, and talents. I outlined how I would use my assets to achieve my goals. I developed a section for accomplished goals, where I wrote them as scrolls and/or scripture for reference and recitation. I developed a working paper on constructing a new life for the benefit of other prisoners beginning a long, hard, and difficult prison journey.

The Purging Process

The Purging Process is an important part of reconstruction. Exploring your past, examination, realization, and cleansing (plucking and healing) are all the essentials that make up its ingredients. I embraced them as mental cleaning and nurturing materials for the internal work I needed to do.

Exploration allows us to explore our past for positive and negative impact experiences. To find ways to read the strong feelings, emotions, or lack thereof, that determine what we become. The examination involves an internal and external inventory. Self-examination analyzes current behavior from past traumatic impacts.

Realization is the beginning stage of the purging process. It is the moment of truth. Coming to terms showed me problem areas that may otherwise not be considered. Through realization/contemplation, the connections can be found between belief systems and behavior patterns and their magnetic correlations.

Realization covers the areas that examine personal liabilities and assets. This kind of examination helps to explore personal faults and inadequacies. Each of us can hide these weaknesses from others but cannot hide these deficiencies from ourselves. I used realization to identify and explore internal resources (capacities, skills, talents, abilities) and, of course, any external resources (family, friends, organizations, religious groups, agencies, etc.).

Acting like a body defense mechanism (T-cell fighters against foreign invaders), cleansing is self-empowerment's corresponding work force. The process involves identifying, categorizing, and breaking down weaknesses to be disposed of by the will of one's own command. Cleansing seeks out for attack negative activities/associations and other consciously identified bad social influences. The process of cleansing will bring renewal, power, and optimism.

Imagination is very important in the plucking and healing process. Imagination houses the power of creativity. Vision to creativity is like the spirit is to the soul. Vision serves as the vehicle upon which creativity rides. Vision brings into focus the creative aspects that mirror our intentions. The body's mechanism is then set up to respond accordingly.

The plucking aspect of cleansing is purely imaginative. These exercises use imaginary procedures to extract unnecessary and excessive waste (negative habits or poor qualities) stored in the subconscious. This plucking process is imaginarily performed before being incorporated into a daily meditation or prayer routine. The emphasis will be enforced through scroll like recitation even after the complete removal of unwanted waste.

After the realization, plucking, and cleansing process, re-harvesting of the mental soil is where the planting of new ideas will take place. Uprooting and disposing of negativity are followed by fertilizing and tranquilizing the mental soil for the harvest of new ideas to take place. The external social element of the plucking process will simply involve an identification and disassociation with bad human influence and other practices designed to stagnate growth and development.

The healing aspect of purging represents the revelation of mental renewal and physical revitalization. It connects me to the source of integrity that serves as a resource for my being. Healing eases my mind and soothes my body with vitality. Healing transmits vibrations of jubilation. It will re-opens clogged physical tunnels and reactivates the natural flow of high energy that is normally detected in a positive aura.

The purging process is irrelevant without action as its application. Purging requires special attention. Preferably the late-night hour timeframe if that's the time that brings quietness. The ions or atomic properties are heavier at night. It makes the mind more perceptive and receptive. The dream state is where problem solving takes place.

Before any self-examination exercise, I would meditate or conduct prayer for calmness, relaxation, and mental clarity. After Medi-prayer, I would follow through with a reflection on the day's activities and then proceed with a self-examination in the manner outlined above. There is a lot to be learnt from these simple exercises. I always wrote down any important observations or discoveries for the purpose of the goal sheet.

The power of belief is also at play. It's simple; if we don't believe it, we probably won't achieve it. Beliefs form value systems and determine behavioral responses to reality. The approach to problem-solving can best be determined through an understanding of one's belief system. If I believed that a bad habit is something that cannot be broken, my inner vision would show me a million ways to become a slave to bad habits.

Spiritual Enhancement

Spiritual Enhancement is the second stage. Like many knowledge seekers, I perceive spirituality through my faith in God. Religious enlightenment and cultural enhancement are two factors that deserve the most credit for individual transformation.

As a vital role in the empowerment process, spirituality must be clearly defined. The traveler will use, adapt, create, or apply their own definition of spirituality on their "Spiritual Enhancement Worksheet" to be used as a framework to guide them on their self-empowerment journey. The answers will differ, but the need for a sense of spirituality is essential. Spirituality will act as the glue that holds everything in place.

I like the concept of spirit being in everything and its relative nature to a divine God source. It helped me to make connections at the mental and physical level. Looking at spirituality in those terms enhanced my understanding and gave me a greater appreciation for just being. It showed me the way in which spirit is the life force that creates us and a power source we can learn to use as a tool. This was one way to bring balance back into my life. Key concepts developed on my spiritual enhancement worksheet were put on a scroll for daily recitation.

Personal Development

Personal Development is the third stage of the self-empowerment process. At the mark of a journey, the travelers must make sense of the distance, possess all the traveling necessities, and know where it is they intend to go in life.

Personal development is the building stage of re-construction. Good health, physical appearance, conduct, and other positive characteristics must radiate. Confidence and determination must be in the driver's seat. Personal development will prepare the traveler with mental and physical toughness. The traveler must be prepared to do all that is necessary to succeed.

To reach this plateau, I would often check my survival kit to make sure everything I need is in my possession. Every traveler will need his or her own personal survival guide. The guide will help the person to understand life's traffic signs, how to yield, when to move, when not to move, and the meaning of other signs left behind by those who have been there before. The personal development chart has a "personal contract" section which describes important personal commitments.

The area of personal development also entails a cultural value system and acquiring skills in interpersonal communication, asset mapping, conceptual and analytical skills, communication skills, computer literacy, journal writing, and other valuable resources. The traveler must put together a tracking system to keep track of accomplished goals and progress.

Sense of Community

The last preparatory stage of my self-empowerment process is to journey with a sense of community. Life journeys may be pursued individually, but when a journey is connected or intersects with another journey, it is no longer a personal endeavor. It becomes a shared event. When personal experiences intertwine, a collective event is formed.

Joint endeavors require working together to complete a task. To travel through an existence that mandates interactive dependency, to a great extent, one must do so with a sense of community. A sense of goodness, willingness, and positive interaction to get through a predicament or situation is all predicated upon a sense of belonging.

We must leave behind as signpost the significant part of our experiences to guide or assist those who follow. It would be unrealistic to start or complete a journey without relying on the wisdom of those who had come before us. If no one left signs of guidance behind, chaos would reign over order. A legacy of order can only be found in a social commitment that improves human relations and protects individual rights.

To travel through life benefiting from others without returning the blessing is unacceptable. A traveler can not truly measure the success of the journey if there is a refusal or failure to leave behind valuable life lessons for others to consider.

Understanding our service to others can be measured in detail against historical reference to trailblazers who left their mark behind. The community component is a responsibility to civic duty.

My social commitment contract application is used to track progress and determine consistency. The value of life, a concern for others, and the need to help change negative conditions that stagnate potential and threaten the future of human survival is based on this social commitment.

Constructing A New Life

The average person will find it ridiculous for anyone to suggest that their state of powerlessness can be seen as their own fault. The fact is most people will spend many years of their life blaming others.

For me, constructing a new life required shattering my old life of powerlessness and/or victimization. Change is the only thing that will bring forth patterns for new realities. But this must first take place in our minds if we are to improve our chance for survival, good health, sanity, and desired results.

Operating from a position of power is the only way to surmount the obstacles of bureaucracy, betrayal, mental anguish, and even physical violence often endemic to failure. The objective of re-constructing a new life was my opportunity to take back my "moment." Life on this plane offers no species a free ride, and all species are only entitled to that moment. It's the only thing life guarantees us!

To construct a new life, I had to first be willing and ready to act. Development requires action. It's simple; the ultimate decision is always made by you. If you don't make that decision, it will be made by another.

Knowing my priorities was important if I was to bring balance back into my life. The priorities I had set determined my survival options and how successful I can become in my goals in transforming my life. I needed to know my priorities to set appropriate goals.

To find my way I had to develop a clear understanding of all the factors that defined my predicament. I begin by asking myself questions about my health, lifestyle, and condition in life. How do I get out of this predicament and what are the things I must do to achieve it? What must I do to take back self-control and use it as a force for resolution?

Survival skills are important. They can determine the course and length of one's travel and the way in which a person's life will unfold. I needed to be aware of my skills in terms of strength to identify my needs for improvement.

Key survival skills should aways begin with maintaining or improving one's health. A complete physical examination and knowledge of the body is essential. Possessing my entire medical record, I used to look deeper into understanding my body's needs.

For proper balance I incorporate an appropriate diet, exercise, and proper rest into my routine. I correlated this approach on the mental and spiritual level through contemplation, recitation, prayer, and the acquisition of useful information relative to achieving my goals.

The tools I needed to survive in a prison setting enabled me to reach my goal beyond expectation. The value of purchasing a jailhouse lawyer's manual and/or a prisoner's self-help litigation manual must not be understated. It is the closest thing to having a lawyer when there is a legal problem.

Established membership and/or relationships with community organization and/or religious group and an attorney, if possible. Community support is a vital resource. I kept a journal or record of important documents, major events, and things of personal interest. I made sure all complaints filed were put in writing, placed in a personal file, and a copy sent home for safekeeping.

The first thing I did was to unlock my mind from the predicament that had seized me. I used books and other outlets to travel historically and culturally and to stay abreast of the changes constantly taking place around me.

On this difficult journey to recovery, I embraced my individuality, my willpower, and the confidence to get the job done. As a rule, never submit to weakness. It's the same as submitting to peer pressure or the negative fads that undermine growth.

Asset mapping was a good way to identify resources or the lack thereof. It gave me a better picture of my resources and helped me to get in touch with my capacities, talents, and abilities to be applied toward accomplishing my goals. I had also developed a brighter picture of my resources, including family/friends, community groups, organizations, and support agencies.

After I completed my inventory, I knew what internal and external resources I had as well as those I would need to empower myself and change my predicament. I used all resources, develop, and established, moral, financial, or advisory for the purposes of the goal.

Irrespective of how small the amount, I learned how to budget my finances, establish good spending and saving habits. I distinguished between my wants and needs and accepted my limitations while looking for way to increase it. If you are not saving and properly investing, you need to reassess how you manage money.

I identify those habits that negatively influenced my life. I added them to my list of goals as things to eliminate. Remember, all unhealthy habits lead to failure. To rid yourself of them will increase your chances of success. Examples of this disease can be found in people who are procrastinators, reactionary, pessimists, operating from a position of powerlessness. They often place blame on others instead of taking responsibility for their own actions or lack thereof.

Before setting goals, I would list my destructive tendencies. I paid particular attention to the primary factors that were nurturing my powerlessness and life of despair.

In developing a goal work sheet, I had to be realistic. My goal setting strategy was to prioritize goals, write them down in an organized manner and stick to my plan. The first and most important goal of all is to develop and maintain excellent physical health.

But to achieve and maintain good health I needed to develop an action plan. This plan involved acquiring knowledge in biology, proper hygiene, and some knowledge in nutrition and proper exercise.

All goals should have a desired result. Mine was to develop health codes and incorporate these codes into a re-constructed lifestyle. The outcome was to eliminate or maintain any health problems.

The first step in the action needed was to get a physical examination. Prepare myself for required research to relevant information in case I had to follow-up on any health issues. Perceiving a goal and reaching it are two different things. Achieving consists of the process or steps taken in a series of actions to accomplish the goal.

The plan is to always make an achieved goal as part of my life obligation. To maintain my focus, I would write my health codes onto a scroll sheet and hang it on the wall for recitation as reinforcement.

Procrastination in fulfilling goals is often due to the lack of prioritization and a reasonable objective time frame. I established a short, intermediate, and long-term timetable to reach my goals. I also incorporated a "to do list," for a suitable time to reach a goal.

I knew, if I failed to complete my list of goals, I would fail to make the most out of my journey. The priorities I set had determined how prepared I would become for my tomorrow. To be successful, the importance of setting goals and maintaining them is the priority.

The best way to find myself during any part of the journey, I would just check my comparative analysis worksheet. It will guide me to where I want to go. I made these comparisons on the pole of polarity by perceiving myself in terms of powerlessness, (takes no responsibility for personal life or the need to change), versus the empowered (takes back responsibility for life while making meaningful self-improvements).

The choices I made to empower myself are not the only choice available to reach that goal. Other people travel different paths. There is no antidote for a guaranteed life of happiness. Human nature confines us to imperfection. That is why I never travel alone. I always wear my *Empowerment shield!*

Making a mental investment is how I turn pain into physical rewards. The price I paid was too harsh to repeat, but the investment I made to persevere was worth it. I stand on this truth as evidence of who I was before I empowered myself and who I have become after doing so.

I am far more knowledgeable than I was before I began my journey, and I am healthier holistically. Yet I still make mental investments, reaping benefits, and I still make mistakes that require corrections.

Internally, self-empowerment requires transformation. Externally, it requires constructing a new life. Change is a vital part of every successfully created self-empowerment process.

The proof of every achievement is in the commitment made and the steps acted upon. Achieving a goal can be determined by the intensity applied. That means staying steadfast, maintaining focus, and executing.

As a seventeen-year-old youth I was determined to educate myself, nurture myself back into excellent mental and physical health, and to walk out of prison under my own terms. The boy who entered the prison system at seventeen was not me the man who left prison at forty-nine years of age.

What a terrible price to pay. I am living proof when I say my abuse at the hands of the criminal justice system was worse than an injustice. It was an act of "deliberate enslavement."

A self-empowerment journey does not guarantee "complete" recovery or success in the pursuit. Prison is an abnormal environment and renders some forms of damage irreversible. My self-empowerment journey is a continuous one that gives me a sense of focus, direction, and balance. It helped me to stay connected with my sanity and to effectively deal with my own challenges.

I obtained a better understanding of myself and discovered some valuable methods to assist in dealing with the madness that redefined my entire existence. I made an investment and benefitted from it.

A SELF-EMPOWERMENT TRANSFORMATION SAMPLE

KNOWING YOUR PRIORITIES
Example:
- Your overall Health.

SURVIVAL SKILLS
Example:
- Self-Defense.

IDENTIFYING YOUR RESOURCES
Example:
- Asset Mapping.

ASSET MAPPING (INTERNAL ASSESSMENT)

CAPACITIES	ABILITIES
Fortitude	Mobilizer
SKILLS	**TALENTS**
Writer	Singer

ASSET MAPPING (EXTERNAL ASSESSMENT)

FAMILY	FRIENDSHIP
Wife	Childhood
SUPPORT GROUPS	**ORGANIZATION**
Religious	The National Trust

BUDGETARY LAYOUT
Example:
- Income divided by Expense (minus needs) equals Saving.

BAD HABITS
Example:
- Procrastination.

LISTING YOUR DESTRUCTIVE TENDENCIES
Example:
- Excessive drug usage.

PRIORITIZE YOUR GOAL WORK SHEET

LIST YOUR MOST IMPORTANT GOALS
Example:
- Excellent Health.

The Action Plan:	Knowledge in Proper Hygiene.
Desired Result:	To Achieve and Maintain good health.
Condition Outcome:	No Major Health Problems.
Actions needed:	A Physical Examination.
Plan:	To Make This Goal a Lifestyle.
Focus:	To do List

TIME FRAME
Short:	Ongoing.
Intermediate:	Ongoing.
Long term:	Ongoing.

REFERRAL SHEET
    To do Today:
    To do this Month:
    To do this Year:

A COMPARATIVE ANALYSIS WORK SHEET

POWERLESSNESS MENTALITY
- Takes no responsibility for personal life; or the need to change.

EMPOWERED MENTALITY
- Takes back responsibility for life while making meaningful self-improvements.

Remember, you have more control over your life than you realize. In problem solving, always example your possibilities. It will lead you to probably solutions and serve as a focal point from which to operate.

INNOCENCE

FOR BEING BLACK, INNOCENT AND POOR
LIFE IMPRISONMENT CONCEALED MY FATE,
TO   PERSIST   IN MY SEARCH FOR EXONERATION,
I RELIED UPON WILL, STRENGTH, AND INNER-FAITH.
RECANTATION CORRUPTION AND NEW   EVIDENCE
WAS DELIBERATELY HIDDEN FROM MY TRIAL JURY,
AFTER 44-PLUS, L-O-N-G YEARS OF DENIALS.
NOW WILL YOU BELIEVE MY STORY!!!

"*EXONEREE KEITH TYRONE BUSH*"

What Freedom Really Feels Like

Freedom is always the goal for those who deeply want it, effort is the only road. If time does not wait for you, surely time will not wait for me, I chose to persist, persist, and persist until I succeeded.

I pushed myself toward mental growth and physical health. I survived over thirty-three years in prison before walking out on my own terms (continuing to maintain my innocence).

I did not leave prison the way I entered. I left highly regarded amongst my peers. I became part of a prison legacy and would imprint my own wisdom on the minds of other prisoners, young and old, by assisting them on their own journeys.

I developed my own self-empowerment approach to help complete the journey.

It was the boy who saw the need to tell this story and initiated the writing of this book. It became my responsibility to finish it.

For forty-plus years, I searched for the truth, and I kept searching until I found it.

The truth that brought me home, I would have never discovered had I not searched. I found it because I was determined and driven by a greater power than myself.

If the criminal justice system had not exonerated me before leaving this earth, I would still have left with the same evidence that exonerated me.

I have always tried to remain in tune with the spiritual side of myself, to rely on intuition and reasoning to find answers as much as I rely on physical evidence.

I have a willingness to dig deep, with the understanding that truth will manifest itself. This is what my legal team and I set out to do.

There were other avenues that required exploration and investigative inquiry. But those who pretended to represent the criminal justice system were not interested in these avenues.

Without the help of experts, professionals, and other people operating within the criminal justice system, the truth would have never been manifested.

My attorney Adele Bernhard and her students had pulled at numerous threads, others have ignored to find the truth.

Some of you may still doubt my innocence regardless of the facts presented in this book. But that is not important. You can believe what you want.

I just hope you do everything you can to protect the rights of all children. What happened to me is still happening today in different, deceptive ways. There will be other victims. I know because I left innocent people behind. Just like me, at the beginning of their journeys, they had no idea of the pain they were about to endure.

If they believe, behave, live, and approach their predicament righteously, they will place themselves in a much better position to persevere. I know this to be true.

Despite my encounter with injustice, there were genuine people who stepped outside of the norm and boldly supported me and my family. The ones who did not know me wanted me to know they were praying for me because they could feel my pain.

There were also two people who once worked within Suffolk County's criminal justice system who tried to help me legally.

The reader must always remember, up until the time of my exoneration, I was hated by people who believed I was guilty of this crime. People have left this world with that same hatred for me. Unfortunately, they did not live long enough to bear witness to the truth. But the future will. This conviction is now a part of the historical records of exoneration and another example of African American enslavement up until the 2019.

This book cost me an extra year in prison for using a computer to tell you, my story! This is a small part of the price I was willing to pay for my freedom.

In addition to all I have presented, I can only hope this book will inspire you to consciously participate in creating the most positive version of who you can become.

Whatever challenges confront you in this sometimes-difficult world, you can overcome.

I have tried my best under the harshest of circumstances to overcome obstacles, tribulations, to find the truth and to stand by its principles. I struggled, lost my way, fell more than once. But I always got back up and never stopped fighting. I am a true Taurean. As stubborn as a bull and determined to challenge those forces that think they had to right to enslave me.

I have suffered the worst. But I still have my sanity. This sanity has driven me on a powerful mission.

That mission was to prove my innocence and seize the desire to know, before my demise, what it really feels like to be *free*.

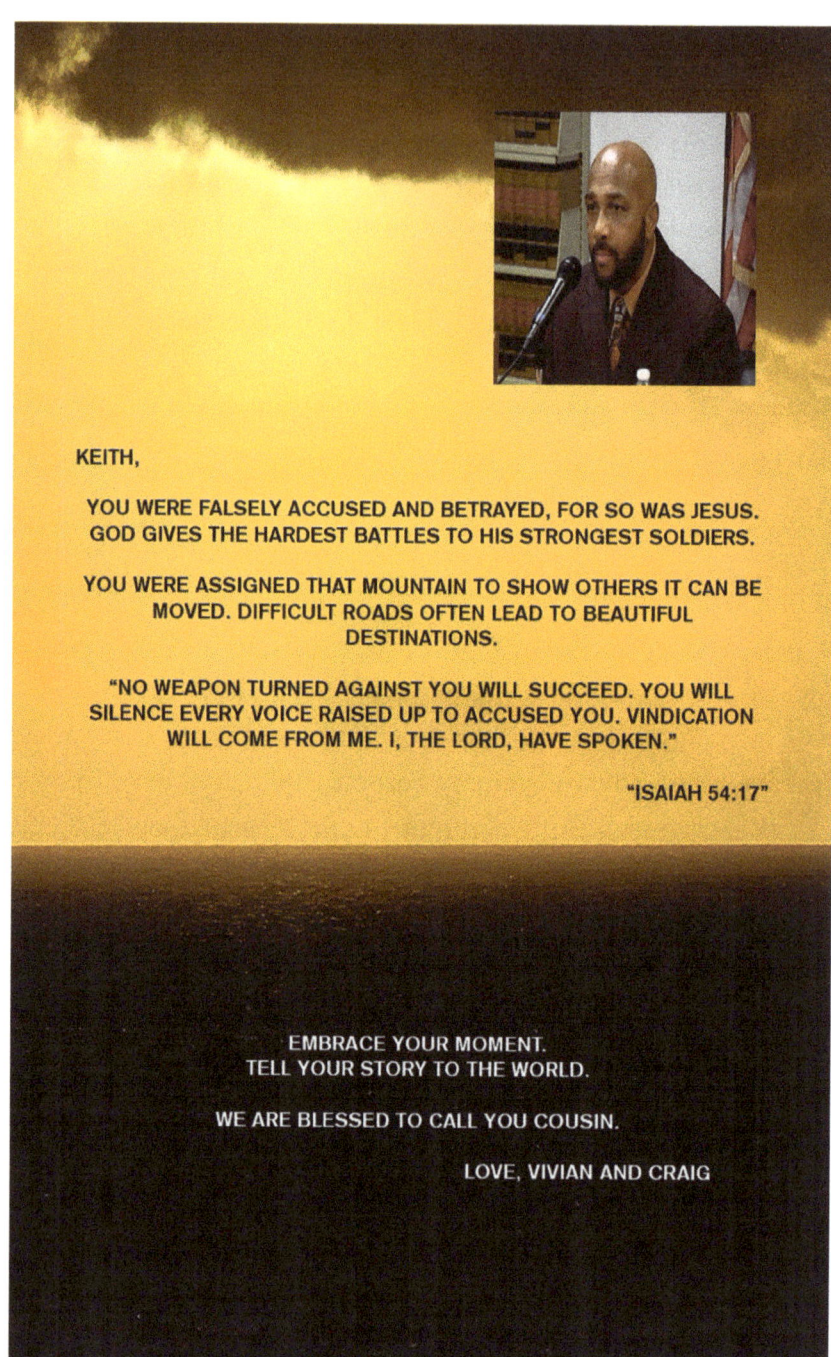

KEITH,

YOU WERE FALSELY ACCUSED AND BETRAYED, FOR SO WAS JESUS. GOD GIVES THE HARDEST BATTLES TO HIS STRONGEST SOLDIERS.

YOU WERE ASSIGNED THAT MOUNTAIN TO SHOW OTHERS IT CAN BE MOVED. DIFFICULT ROADS OFTEN LEAD TO BEAUTIFUL DESTINATIONS.

"NO WEAPON TURNED AGAINST YOU WILL SUCCEED. YOU WILL SILENCE EVERY VOICE RAISED UP TO ACCUSED YOU. VINDICATION WILL COME FROM ME. I, THE LORD, HAVE SPOKEN."

"ISAIAH 54:17"

EMBRACE YOUR MOMENT.
TELL YOUR STORY TO THE WORLD.

WE ARE BLESSED TO CALL YOU COUSIN.

LOVE, VIVIAN AND CRAIG

Photo Gallery

Basketball Champions 1973

Date of Arrest

Elmira Prison 1976

Mother's maternal line, Long Island Native American bloodline of the Setauket and Shinnecock nations.

The first photo is the personification of my father, Francis Raymond Bush Sr. He is seen here with his niece Wendy. My father (Ray) had a personality like no other. He lived his life on his own terms and bowed to no one. Brutally violent in rage or jealousy, he was also amicable, loved and respected by his peers. My father was a Hercules. He was a little man with the status, power, and strength of a giant.

Sister Raynese Bush.   Raynese with my baby sister   Madeline Bush

Ray Jr., Me, Mother and Mark

Mark, me and Calvin Robinson

Me, My Brothers, A Cousin and Four Nephews

Death row exoneree the late Anthony Peek with wife. Peek used to ask me to write letters he wanted to read on the gate to death row prisoners to help uplift their spirits.

Some of the core members who built one of the most successful empowerment programs in the country, *"The Resurrection Study Group."* From left to right: Dr. Ronald Day; Lorenzo (Rakim) Brooks; Keith Bush; Stanley (Jamel) Bellamy; Joseph Robinson; Charles (Hasson) Gales; Dr. Andre (Imani) Ward; and Kenny Innis.

Dr. Alice Green, Exec. Dir., The Center for Law & Justice, played a pivotal role in establishing the Green Haven Annual Legislative Conferences and promoting the NTA analysis.

Me giving a presentation to members of the New York State Black Legislative Caucus during the 2nd Legislative Conference.

Members of the Black NYS Legislators at the 2nd Annual Legislative Conference (February 1991)

Stepfather Tom Bolling with Mother. A great stepfather and one of my strongest supporters.

MOTHER'S 85th BIRTHDAY PARTY

Setauket tribal leader Helen Sells, Mother and Uncle Melvin. Last of their generation.

Me, Minister Chaplin and Master G.   Gerald, Mark, Vinny and Rhonda

Mother's oldest niece, Elaine Mc Allister, addressing the family.

A spiritual tribute to an Earth Queen.

Mother's oldest grandson, Fatman, reading a special plate in her honor.

Giving a tribute to my Mother on her 85th birthday.

Some family members who attended the party.

Your so-called experts underestimated me. Your system of justice abused me and then threw me in a cage to die. I only did what every human being is obligated to do **FIGHT BACK!** There is no love or allegiance to those who think they have the right to enslave me. I was prepared to fight until my last breath of life!

The National Innocent Network 2024 annual Conference.

Dora and me on a cruise in 2024

www.ingramcontent.com/pod-product-compliance
Lightning Source LLC
LaVergne TN
LVHW061530070526
838199LV00009B/434